The Violi

A felon with a difficult and tumultuous past tells his life story at a state prison reform symposium. He remembers, at about age 8, when he, his mother and younger sister, abandoned by her live-in boyfriend, moved to an inner-city neighborhood in Ogden, Utah.

Although the transition was difficult from their previous home in remote Montana, he soon realized all the opportunity available to him, most of an unsavory "finding" nature. He started by finding a wardrobe off the clothes lines in backyards throughout the neighborhood.

Looking for a faster way to get around, he found a bicycle to ride. Soon he realized that "finding" bikes had a monetary value and that multiple buyers were willing to pay for his entrepreneurial efforts.

Before long, he made his first trip to juvenile court. Those visits to court were frequent for the next few years. By age 14, he was in and out of juvenile detention. At age 17, he did his first jail time. The trend continued and he received his first prison sentence just before he turned 20 for distribution of a controlled substance.

At age 29, he'd been in and out of prison three times. Now, once again, he stood before the judge, about to return to prison for the fourth time. He was angry. More importantly, the judge was disgusted.

Just before passing sentence, the judge asked him if he had anything to say.

"Yeah," he said. "Can I ask you a question?"

"What?" replied the judge.

"Can I ask you a question?"

"What is it?" the judge responded impatiently.

Looking down at his feet and then back up at the judge, the young man asked, "Can you play the violin?"

i

"No," came the response.

"What if I told you that you have to play *The Star-Spangled Banner* on the violin. Could you do it?"

Again, came the response, an emphatic, "No!"

"What if I put a gun to your head and threatened to pull the trigger if you failed to play *The Star-Spangled Banner*. Could you do it?"

"No! What's the point?" decried the judge.

"And if I threatened your family, could you play it then?"

Completely impatient, the judge nearly shouted, "No! I can't play the violin under any circumstances. I never learned how. What is the point?"

Again, looking at the ground in front of him, the convicted drug dealer quietly responded, "I don't know how to live a good life. Can you teach me?"

From that exchange, the judge determined that this man lacked understanding of how to live an honest, honorable life. Rather than sentence him to prison for the fourth time, he placed him in a rehab program with certain requirements and limitations.

To finish the story, that exchange with the judge was eight years prior to the state ASCENT symposium where the felon was speaking.

The former inmate now has a family: a beautiful wife with two children. He owns a business and is a positive contributor to society and has been for more than six years.

This painting of a violin hangs in the hallway of the Education corridor of the Central Utah Correctional Facility in Gunnison, Utah. It was painted by an inmate I nicknamed "Rembrandt." It is a reminder to inmates, teachers, and officers that felons can change.

All My Friends Are Felons

Finding Hope for the Utah Department of Corrections

Mark Hugentobler, B.S., M.A., A.S.C.

Impact books with a message!

ISBN: 978-1-7339407-5-7

©Copyright 2020 Mark Hugentobler

1-8560013081

Cover illustration by an inmate

Library of Congress Control Number: 2020903654

First printing 2020

DEDICATION

This book is dedicated to Dan Adams, (1962-2011) who was a model husband, father and friend. Without his inspirational friendship, I would have never had the courage to attempt this undertaking.

We often forget the other victims of criminal behavior – the parents, the spouses and the children of the perpetrator. This book is also dedicated to them as well as to the many inmates who possess a strong desire to change and become productive people.

All the author's proceeds from this book are donated to Bridges Charities, a non-profit organization whose mission it is to help the aforementioned bridge the gap to becoming productive, successful members of our society. www.bridgescharities.org

Special Thanks

I can't thank enough the many people who contributed to this book. That includes the writings of three currently incarcerated men who were willing to share their stories, as well as artwork from two inmates. (All their names have been changed in the book). In addition, Brian Wood, a former inmate, has made major contributions not only in writing but in listening and providing his input.

Finally, I need to thank several family members and friends, namely my wife, Angie, daughter Emily (who hopes to one day be an editor) my sister-in-law Melanie and several friends who read and proofed the manuscripts offering their insight and expertise. Their contributions have been vital to this publication.

Preface

We are all broken. That's how the light gets in.
                                    – Ernest Hemingway

Though I truly loved my job in the prison, in the spring of 2019 I made the decision to retire. I had spent 34 years in the Education system, the last eight working at the Central Utah Academy (CUA), inside Central Utah Correctional Facility (CUCF) in Gunnison, Utah.

My wife and I were on our way to Cedar City, Utah, to attend the annual Adult Education Directors Meeting and were reminiscing on my previous eight years. I had so many stories and experiences and names. It was enjoyable. As I thought through the many events of those eight years I suggested to my wife that it seemed that all my friends are felons. Along the conversation, Angie mused that I ought to write a book. We both laughed while contemplating the possibility.

Our trip to southern Utah included a visit to the Washington County Correctional Facility, Purgatory. Several years prior, inside CUCF, we started a computer coding program for the inmates that we later shared with several county jails throughout the state. Purgatory was one of those facilities. I wanted to go and support their new computer coding venture.

As I entered the jail and made my way through security, the director and I walked into the large classroom. At the desk in the corner sat the inmate tutor. I immediately recognized him as a previous student from CUCF. He greeted me warmly and we visited about his life since CUCF. A short time later, the classroom began to fill with student/inmates, about 25 or so. Among them I recognized a half dozen, knowing four by name. When they saw me, they all approached and expressed their appreciation that I had come to visit. After that exchange, I turned to the director and with a wry look on my face said, "All my friends are felons." His response was immediate, "That sounds like the perfect title for a book."

Several hours later as I climbed back in the car, I told my wife of that exchange and well, here we are. I determined to write a book.

I truly appreciate all the people who have contributed to this writing. I count the eight years I spent working in the Central Utah Correctional Facility (CUCF) as being key to gaining insights into the perspectives and situations faced by Corrections administration, Corrections officers, Education staff and inmates.

Nowhere is it my intent to discredit or disparage anyone who may be included in this book, either by name or position. My eight years "down" have given me incredible insights from many perspectives into the condition of the Utah Department of Corrections (UDOC). As a noncertified staff member (not an officer), I had the opportunity to work closely with offenders. It was not uncommon to have one or more of them in my office addressing the many challenges we faced. Inmates came to trust me and speak openly with me. Likewise, I garnered great relationships with many Correctional officers. Their insights, frustrations, and hope – or lack thereof – came out clearly in our conversations.

Though the contents of this book may upset some of the UDOC leadership, I am confident that the majority of officers I worked with at CUCF will welcome and agree with its contents and conclusions.

Because I'm a bit of a maverick, I made several trips to the capitol. I had conversations with the Utah Lieutenant Governor as well as several state legislators. Most recently, I was privileged to have a valued conversation with the Executive Director of the UDOC. Most of these conversations made me feel I was speaking with someone who cared and wanted to make a difference. However, because of their perspective, the limitations they see and perhaps not seeing from the inside as I do, little of value happened for change, at least from my view.

Many outstanding Correctional officers work throughout the system. The large majority of the people that I met and worked with in my eight years at the Central Utah Correctional Facility (CUCF) were professionals doing the very best they could, given their circumstance and situation. I make the same claim for all the educators past and present who worked at the Central Utah Academy (CUA), the adult Education program located inside CUCF. Their desired efforts have been commendable. And finally, the many inmates with whom I had the opportunity to work closely, have a strong desire for an opportunity to change and a way to find hope. I was amazed, as they worked and developed in our programs, at how many of them grew and changed and began to realize a better way to live.

Unfortunately, I cannot say the same thing for the system. The best way to describe the bureaucracy that is the UDOC is the tail wagging the dog. To effect real change, that must be resolved.

These experiences have shown me that many, even the majority, of inmates in the Correctional system would change if a system of rehabilitation could be developed to provide that change. I don't believe they will all change. Some of them refuse to ever want to find a better way to live. This book does not address those attitudes; only those who seek to improve their lives will do so.

Interestingly, as stated above, I do not believe the people who work in Corrections are bad people or necessarily derelict. I have met many of these people and have found them to be, as much as in any other profession, people of integrity who want to do their job to the best of their ability. I believe that the fault lies in the strong tradition of a system that was originally set up as a punishment system. The efforts to morph it into a Correctional system have been well-intended, but ineffective.

The impetus for the ideas presented in this book comes from two sources. The first is the excellent ASCENT directive sent down from the Governor's office to restructure and reform the UDOC, presented in a symposium the summer of 2016. The second comes from working with the many inmates, Corrections staff, and CUA teachers and staff.

I want to emphasize here that I am not justifying the inmates incarcerated in the UDOC. They have hurt people and deserve to be incarcerated. They have lost their right to be in society. The things they have done are reprehensible. I do not condone any of them. I cannot imagine how I would feel if someone I loved was victimized by one of these men. It would be incredibly difficult to resolve at a personal level. This book does not address a felon's debt to society nor the intense personal damage they have done to so many people. That is not for me to decide and I don't want to minimize that or eliminate it.

The purpose of this book can easily be stated as a concentrated effort to address the many facets of a failed Corrections system that continues, instead of being a true Corrections system, to be a punitive prison system. I hope to suggest viable, practical, inexpensive and effective solutions.

Albert Einstein said, "Learn from yesterday, live for today, hope for tomorrow. The important thing is not to stop questioning."

There is great value in that statement if one wishes to change anything for the better. My hope is that this writing explores important questions and proposes some viable and valuable answers to questions that need to be asked.

Finally, I want to pre-apologize to anyone who may be offended by the content of this book. It is not my intent to disparage anyone personally. Yet I realize this may happen.

Sometimes getting to the bottom of a mess requires telling truths that people don't like to hear. I believe that will be the case in this writing. It is not my desire to become contrary. To quote Victor Hugo, "to be ultra is to go beyond ... it is to champion things to the point of becoming their enemy, it is to become so pro you become con." I hope to not become so pro that I become con.

Most names in this work are fictional.

Let penitentiaries be turned into seminaries of learning. Rigor and seclusion never do as much to reform the propensities of men as [would] reason and friendship.

Joseph Smith

Often we forget that before they fell into criminal behavior, many of these men led more "normal" lives. Though different in detail, their stories have the potential to help us understand how they ended up in prison. Space does not allow us to include these experiences in this book. We have gathered several of these "biographies" and you can read them on our website, bridgescharities.org

Prison Vernacular

As we have gone through the writing of this project, we have discovered many parts of the Utah Department of Corrections puzzle with which most people are unfamiliar. Before I went to the prison, I had absolutely no idea how prisons operated, their layout, their hierarchy, etc. So, with this section, we hope to remove some of that ambiguity, at least as it relates to this documentation. This information relates directly to the existing prison system in Utah, specifically to CUCF.

Acronyms:
- **CUCF** – Central Utah Correctional Facility located at Gunnison Utah. Houses approximately 1,700 inmates.
- **CUA** – Central Utah Academy. The Adult Education program inside CUCF. Provides services towards improving Adult Basic Education skills, high school graduation, GED attainment. Currently there are 12 teachers, 1 administrator, 2 secretaries and 1 counselor. It is located inside a corridor in CUCF in which there are 10 classrooms, a testing center, a tutor room where curriculum is created and all processes are evaluated and controlled, 2 closed-circuit TV Stations are produced and all the SIS systems are maintained. This is the hub of CUA.
- **AP&P** – Adult Probation and Parole – the parole officers who monitor paroled inmates
- **ABE** – Adult Basic Education level.
- **SIS** – Student Information System. We named ours InfoNet and Inmate Summary

- **GED** – General Education Development test – Equivalent to a high school diploma
- **TABE** – Test of Adult Basic Education. A standardized test that evaluates the Adult Basic Education grade level of each individual.
- **UPA** - Utah Preparatory Academy – A post-secondary academy we established that provides post-secondary education opportunities for inmates. Participation requires successful completion and graduation from CUA or equivalent. Courses include everything from Basic Study Skills to Math 1500. Until the UDC canceled it, there existed an extensive building trades program as well.
- **UPrep** – Another common name for UPA.
- **UCI** – Utah Correctional Industries. This is the official business arm of the UDC. At CUCF, UCI had a sign shop and a sewing shop.
- **OMR** – Offender Management Review. A weekly meeting held by the officer leadership of each housing unit in which they dealt with the many issues, positive and negative, of inmates housed in their respective housing units.
- **PML** – Permission Matrix Level. An inmate's PML is earned with good or poor behavior. It allows the UDC to identify at a glance what access inmates can have, what time they must be back in their housing unit and cell, what commissary is allowed, etc. Each individual inmate is assigned a PML. Their PML goes up and down depending on behavior.
- **PS** – Programming Sergeant. Also referred to as a Caseworker. These officers dealt with a specific group of inmates within their respective housing unit. There were typically 2 per unit.
- **IPP** – Inmate Placement Program. This is the "tail that wags the dog." This organization was put in

place to identify and select inmates to be placed in the various county jails throughout Utah. Typically selected to go to county are the best behaved, most productive inmates to move to county because they posed the smallest threat. Except for "Captain," IPP was the scariest thing to most inmates. Very few wanted to be shipped to county. One even stated to me that he would rather do one year at CUCF rather than 6 months at county.

- **IPP'd** – The process of being "rolled up" or sent out from Draper or CUCF to a county jail.
- **HOPE** – Helping Offenders Parole Effectively – A drug rehab program in CUCF. Though well intentioned, as one inmate told me, "If you go in an honest man, you won't be when you come out."
- **LSAC** – Licensed Substance Abuse Counselor. These counselors serve as part of the HOPE program.
- **RRG** – Remedial Reform Group. This is a part of the discipline portion of the HOPE program.
- **STRIVE** – Strength Through Responsibility, Integrity, Values and Effort. A program in the Gale Housing Unit that required each inmate to do 40 hours per week of productive time and used incentives to reward positive behavior and progress. This is a program started by a Captain of her own initiative. It receives very little to no additional funding. It is the most effective UDC program for helping inmates to change. The current Captain claims a 10% recidivism rate for inmates who parole from STRIVE. This is by far the best UDC program in the system.
- **SMU** – Special Management Unit. A very secure area where inmates are sent, (usually temporarily) after an incident for evaluation and safety, etc.
- **STG** - Severe Threat Group. Used to identify those inmates with gang affiliation, past or present.

- **R&O** – Receiving and Orientation. When he first comes into prison, every inmate spends multiple weeks in R&O.
- **UDC** – Utah Department of Corrections.
- **UDOC** - Utah Department of Corrections.
- **UDP** – Utah Department of Prisons.
- **UDOWD** – Utah Defendant/Offender Workforce Development Task Force. It is the UDC transition program.
- **DWS** – Utah's Department of Workforce Services.
- **USOE** – Utah State Office of Education.
- **USBE** – Utah State Board of Education. This is the new name for the USOE.
- **UA** – Urine Analysis. A method of testing an individual for drug use.
- **LWOP** – Life Without Parole.

Locations:
- **The Ivory Tower** – The Fred House Academy in Salt Lake City. The Prison's administration complex across I-15 from The Draper Prison.
- **The house** – How inmates often refer to their respective cells.
- **Medical** – Where inmates received medical treatment.
- **The Henrys** – A group of 4 housing Units in a single building within a confined fence/area of CUCF.
- **The Boulders** – A group of 4 housing units in a single building within a confined fence/area of CUCF.
- **The Monroes** – Contains a single housing unit within a confined fence/area. It is the name of the newest addition of CUCF.
- **Housing Unit** – Separate units where inmates are housed.

- **Section** – Each housing unit is separated into 3-6 sections of 50 – 160 inmates.
- **Yard** – An outdoor area where inmates can play various sports and activities.
- **Mini Yard** – a small area within each housing unit for exercise.
- **Dogwood** – The official name for SMU.
- **Aspen** – A housing unit in the Henries.
- **Birch** - A housing unit in the Henries.
- **Cedar** - A housing unit in the Henries.
- **Elm** - A housing unit in the Boulders.
- **Fir** - A housing unit in the Boulders. Inmates in this housing unit are participating in the HOPE drug rehab program.
- **Gale** - A housing unit in the Boulders. Inmates in this housing unit are participating in the STRIVE personal development program. This is a dorm-style housing unit laid out more like an army barracks than a prison. Cells have been replaced with cubicles. Inmates in GALE are functioning at a much higher level that most other inmates in CUCF.
- **Hickory** - A housing unit in the Boulders. Inmates in this housing unit are on a very restricted status either for their behavior or their safety.
- **Ironwood** – A housing unit in the Monroes. This is the newest housing unit in CUCF. Most of these inmates are workers and function at a reasonably mature level.

General Definitions:
- **Tutor** – An inmate that works for Education either as a teacher tutor or in the tutor room. They are critical to education success.

- **Facilitator** – An inmate who works for Education as a class director. They provide after-hour help and instruction to fellow inmates both in the Education corridor and in the some of the housing units.
- **OutReach** – An after-hours Education program developed to provide help and instruction to inmates. Outreach classes were taught after hours in the education corridor as well as at all hours of the day in several housing units.
- **InfoNet** – A Student Information System (SIS) developed by several inmates that provides a complete set of educational information for each inmate housed in CUCF. It allows Education, Programming, Sergeants and Corrections leadership to have up-to-the-day accurate information about inmate individual schedules, progress, education compliance and eligibility for employment.
- **Inmate Summary** – The version of InfoNet pushed out to the appropriate Corrections staff.
- **Education** – A common way to refer to the CUA corridor as well as its many other facets and operation.
- **Programming** – Refers to the various courses offered by Corrections in which officers are the instructors. Courses like Victim Impact and Thinking for a Change are taught. Also includes any other "educational program" provided under the Corrections umbrella such as HOPE, CONQUEST, and Education.
- **Corrections** – A common way to refer to the Utah Department of Corrections.
- **ASCENT** – A program rolled out by the governor's office in search of a way to improve the prison system and move it into a more of a Corrections system.

- **Fish or Fished In** – This is what new prisoners are often referred to.
- Being **Down** – Being in prison.
- On the **Outs** – Being released from prison.
- **The House** – How inmates refer to their cell.
- **Slider** – Term for a door that slides. Sliders are opened by an officer who monitors from a bubble.
- **Popper** – Term for a door that opens on hinges much like a normal door. Poppers are opened by an officer who monitors from a bubble.
- **Recidivism** – The tendency of a convicted criminal to re-offend.

The Hierarchy

The Executive Director – Appointed by the Governor, this person oversees all operations of the UDC and UDP.

Deputy Director – Individuals who support the Executive Director in his duties.

Warden – Every prison has a warden.

Deputy Warden – Individuals who support the Prison Warden in his duties.

Captain – Each prison has many captains, each one with a different responsibility. Captains are given enormous leeway in the method in which they run their responsibility.

- Duty Captain – One captain who manages the day-to-day challenges of the prison.
- Housing Unit Captain
- Programming Captain
- Kitchen Captain
- MEGA Captain
- Etc.

Lieutenants – Serve under their respective captains.

Sergeants – Serve many functions but they answer directly to their lieutenants.

Officers – Similar to privates in the army. They perform the day -to-day operations of the prison.

Contents

Chapter 1

Utah Department of Corrections Mission Statement

*"Our dedicated team of professionals ensures public safety by effectively managing offenders while maintaining close collaboration with partner agencies and the community. **Our team is devoted to providing maximum opportunities for offenders to make lasting changes through accountability, treatment, education, and positive reinforcement** within a safe environment."*

Currently, 70% of inmates released from the Utah Department of Corrections return to prison. This is among the highest rates of return, or recidivism, of prison systems in the United States. Statistically, 33% of the inmates would self-correct simply because they have "learned their lesson." Shown by these numbers, the current system has a *net negative* effect on reducing the number of returning offenders.

Obviously, the prison population grows because there are too many going in and too few coming out. The majority of those entering prison in 2017 were not being sent there for committing a crime, but instead for breaking parole or probation rules. In that year, an astounding 79% of those going into prison were those returning as a result of parole or probation violations, not re-offenses. Some 53% of them had been released to parole, violated that parole, and were sent back to prison. Offenders sentenced to probation by the courts and later returned to prison for failing their probation made up the additional 26%.

As of August, 2019, Utah had 6,741 people in prison. If recidivism were even moderately under control —say, at 50%, we would have only 4,044 people in the prison system. The difference, in practical terms, is the waste of hundreds of millions of dollars. In Utah today, recidivism is not under control.

The largest contributor to recidivism is addiction. Hundreds of people with addictions have returned to prison more than fifteen times, the highest group of recidivism. The principal underlying cause of their recidivism is the failure to properly manage and effectively treat addictions.

The system is bleeding from the femoral artery and they are trying to save patients with a Band-Aid.

Over 95% of incarcerated individuals will eventually be released. Though these people may or may not deserve help, not helping them is foolish. The financial waste of doing nothing is astounding. If we do nothing, the cost continues to rise. They will eventually be "back on the streets." The hurt caused by these people continues to be perpetuated; the wasted human resource goes unchecked.

I believe we can do better.

This brings up another point. I also want to ask why, because these men have done terrible harm to others to the point of incarceration, are they ever released early before they have changed?

Why can't we create a system that requires not only their debt to be paid, but also truly rehabilitates the inmates? I'm not talking about a bunch of hoops to jump through in the last six months of incarceration or "getting a time cut" for doing this program or that. That's the current system which is very unproductive, as shown by the statistics. I'm talking about a real pathway to change that requires a marked, established process. Such a process would require *years* of constant effort and accountability by individuals, both inmates and Corrections staff. It would require a dramatic change in the current system. Importantly, it would not cost a great deal to the taxpayer. The biggest challenge would be to change the traditional culture of the UDOC, which follows a punitive path. It currently lacks a common direction and completely ignores its own mission statement.

I know from personal experience that this punitive system, though steeped in many years of tradition, can be changed. I have been involved in a group for the past eight years that has not just imagined a viable pattern of systematic change, but has enacted that change using mostly inmate resources. Everything we have accomplished has come at NO additional cost to the Utah Department of Corrections.

In 2011, just over 200 students were enrolled in the prison school in Gunnison, Utah, the Central Utah Academy (CUA).

As of March, 2019, we hosted 1,027 students. In 2011, 24 computers were available for student use. Now there are 142. In 2011, we were one of the smaller adult education programs in the State of Utah, dwarfed by Jordan Adult Ed, Granite Peaks Adult Ed and Horizonte Adult Ed. Currently we are the third largest program with more than 1,000 students. In 2011, Education from both the inmates' perspective as well as Corrections' perspective, was a hiss and a byword. In 2019 we were an integral and valued part of each housing unit and a place of hope and opportunity for the inmates.

The growth described is more than a statistic or a number; it is based in real outcomes that are a result of real change. That change was effected not just in the culture of our school's faculty and staff but also, and more importantly, in the nature of the students and inmate tutors. More than once I've had an inmate in my office complaining that he doesn't need education or that he is too old or making some other lame excuse only to have him in my office some 6-8 months later thanking me for the experience he had. The inmates felt encouraged by the changes they made and the accomplishments they achieved.

The statistical outcomes are a result of an ongoing cultural change on the part of all old as well as new stakeholders.

That growth didn't come without a great deal of pain and work. The biggest change occurred on the attitudes of the housing unit leadership, of the academy's faculty and staff and finally the inmates housed at the Gunnison prison.

I have been amazed as I have been a part of such a change, creating hope, a clear path, opportunity, accountability and positive outcomes for individuals. I believe that what we did could be implemented on an even larger scale to positively affect countless lives for the better. I am confident, if done correctly, it could be implemented throughout the Gunnison prison (CUCF) with very little additional cost to the taxpayer, and in the long run, bring substantial savings.

Perhaps a total restructure is impractical. Some may say it's too expensive. Some may say the lawyers will ruin any effort to effect real change. Others may blame the Corrections staff, while many others don't really care. However, the financial cost to the State of Utah is currently astounding. In 2015, the expenditures for the Utah Department of Corrections was more than $152 million. That equates to roughly $28,000 per inmate per year.

If we could reduce the state recidivism rate by even 10%, that savings would be in the neighborhood $15 million annually. That is just the up-front financial savings. This does not include additional court costs, or expenses and suffering of victims, and it certainly does not include the loss to humanity suffered by the citizenry in general, and the inmates in particular. Imagine if we could achieve 20-30%

4

reduction in recidivism. In my mind it is worth a discussion; thus, the purpose of this book.

The above information was provided by Utah Prison Advocacy Network (UPAN) to illustrate the current situation of recidivism in Utah prisons. You may also like to reference an article in *The Salt Lake Tribune*, https://www.sltrib.com/news/politics/2019/05/28/all-utahs-justice/

Imagine
Hope lies in dreams, in imagination, and in the courage of those who dare to make dreams into reality....

Jonas Salk

Imagine your perspective if you are the one who is incarcerated: You have done something terrible to others and fully deserve it. You may have grown up "on the streets" or may have had a good life that you threw away because of some terrible choices. You are now stuck behind bars. You want to change but everything around you prevents it. Everywhere you look there is rampant corruption. You feel like you are living in a cesspool. Every day you worry that you will anger the wrong person, inmate or guard. Every day you wonder if this will be the day that you are beat up or thrown in Special Management Unit (SMU, a secure holding cell), sent to a county jail or worse. Every time you dare think you can change and make the attempt to do so, the reality of where you are, and all the obstacles, including the "system" are staring you down.

Imagine you are a guard: getting up every day with no hope. Imagine going to work every day knowing full well that the environment where you are going is hopeless and meaningless. In the beginning you had hope. You are charged to guard inmates. You imagined you could make a difference. You thought that you could help. After a short time, however, you realized that the system and the environment are too overwhelming to do anything positive. Every time you try, you run into a roadblock within the system. You are criticized for trying to create meaningful change. You are told that it won't make a difference. You are told that those you wanted to help don't deserve it. You are considered a traitor because of the "us vs them" attitude that prevails at your work place. You are stuck in a job that provides little in the way of positive outcome for you or for the people you are supposed to be serving. You spend your day in boredom.

Now imagine my perspective as an educator and seeing 1,500 students who need help, lots of help. Many of these students made grave mistakes. Most have done serious damage to someone or something. Many were remorseful but saw no clear path to correcting their behavior. In fact, they are living in a world that encourages and develops criminal behavior. Imagine being there with your "students" and having your hands tied. Your responsibility to help is real. However, because of a broken system, you are not allowed to do anything positive. You come every day to work with 200 students who are mostly passive. You know full well that there are many, many more out there who need your help, though they may not want it. Your predecessors told you that you would have nothing to do, that you would spend your days reading the paper and standing in the hall during "movement" of prisoners between classes. They advised you to keep your door closed so as to not invite the "students" in.

Imagine, through either providence or sheer dumb luck, that, you as an educator, find your way to help all these parties see a better path. In your daily interaction with these "students" and their jailors, as well as your faculty and staff – eliciting the help of all – you are able to see the many flaws

6

in the current system and develop a program that, in a small way, opens the path and opportunity of growth for many of them. Imagine a grown man, 58 years old, standing in the doorway of your office pitching a fit because he had to come to school. Then imagine him two and a half years later as he stands in the same doorway, this time in tears, thanking you and your staff for the opportunity of learning. For the first time in his life he felt he has hope for the future. Imagine an officer, who at the beginning of your tenure, was critical and mocking as you started to try to make change. Now he comes to see you before you retire, thanking you for the positive effect the changes have had on those with whom he worked, as well as on himself. He was dreading the "next 15 years" but now comes to work with hope and a vision.

This is an account of how our group of teachers, inmates and some Corrections staff, over the course of eight years, effected real change inside the Gunnison prison (CUCF).

Unfortunately, this change is likely a passing phenomenon. The current system is completely ineffective, in fact, it is detrimental. It doesn't make people better; it actually makes them worse. It is sad because with some simple changes in paradigm, some real changes in priorities with very little or no money, things could be different.

Changing the prison system to a Correctional system will take a change in attitude and focus. But it will take very little money. In fact, over time, by reducing the number of inmates returning to prison, it would save millions of dollars.

Here's how it could be changed. It is possible because nowhere in the world is there a more "controlled" student population. Imagine a world where people who were severely broken were required to change **before** they were paroled. Imagine a Corrections system that required achievement and progress from people before they could move from their current situation to a situation in which they had further opportunity for growth. Imagine a system where an individual would start at point A, successfully complete

7

specific requirements and then move on to B, then C, then D. At each step, they would have to demonstrate changed behavior before moving on. And after each step, their environment would change, moving them away from the criminal world that is the current system, into a better and better physical, social, and emotional situation. As they progress, they would move from the cesspool that is the general population in the current prison system to a level where, though incarcerated, they live in a civil society in a controlled environment practicing the social skills and soft skills required to get along. At the same time, they would be developing employability skills. Imagine if they could identify their inappropriate thoughts and behaviors, accept where they are, and make logical, effective steps to overcoming those. Imagine a system that tailors the rehab to the individual. Imagine parole being granted only to those who achieve certain levels. It would not be near as difficult as the powers that be imagine.

Imagine.

Chapter 2

My Sentence

Life is what happens to you
when you're making other plans.

John Lennon

"I didn't sign up to work with inmates! I signed up to help teenagers. I have zero interest!" That was the answer I gave in 2011 when one of my peers, the principal at another school in our school district, inquired as to my interest in the recently vacated job of principal of Central Utah Academy, (CUA), a school located within the Central Utah Correctional Facility (CUCF).

The offer came because I worked for the South Sanpete School District. In addition to two high schools, two middle schools and three elementary schools, this school district also oversees the Educational program inside the state Correctional facility in Gunnison, Utah.

The principal of this facility had been asked to take responsibility at a local junior high, leaving open the position as principal at CUA. It remained open because few educators in the area had interest in working at the little prison school. Most of the dozen or so teaching positions inside the facility likewise garnered little interest. At the time, most positions at the CUA were taken by teachers to get started in the district when no other positions were available, or a few who were deliberately moved out of the public-school system.

I had worked at Manti High School, a rural school in central Utah, for about fifteen years. Most of those years I was the boys' basketball coach, athletic director and algebra teacher. For the last three years, I was the assistant principal.

Three months later, I was in my office at school working on attendance. Two days remained in the school year and I was finishing up my yearly reports when the phone rang. It was my superintendent asking me to come to his office before the end of the day. At 2 p.m. I made the short drive and walked in his office. The look on his face told me this wasn't going to be an easy conversation.

"Mark," he said, with a pinched look in his eye, "you are being sent to the prison to be the principal." He went on to explain that it was "the board's" doing. I was dumbfounded. Usually I have an inkling of a "catastrophic" event coming my way. Heaven knows I've done my share of dumb stuff. But this – well, I was completely oblivious, despite many warning signs.

I entered into education to coach high school basketball. It had been a dream of mine since I was in my teens. I greatly admired several of my coaches and even though I had great parents, siblings and friends, some of my high school coaches had a lasting influence on me. My family taught me to get outside myself and get over myself. They taught me hard work and dedication and teamwork. They taught me to love life and find the best. Being a slow learner, I also needed important life skills reinforced by my coaches as I participated in football, basketball and track.

Following my dream, I earned the necessary degrees, and, for the next twenty-three years, pursued the adventurous life of a high school basketball coach. I truly enjoyed my job and some say that I was even fairly good at it. In fact, before retiring, I had spent 34 years in the education business and only had about 3 years when I didn't look forward to going to work. I truly loved what I did. Referring to my happiness as a coach, my wife once referenced it as "a pig living in stink." Not sure how that applies? Anyway, coaching was my passion. I worked with many great players and they all made a big impact on me. I'm hoping I helped them as I had been helped by my coaches when I was a kid.

Yet coaching in a small town can be complicated, especially when it comes to basketball. Basketball coaches estrange a lot of people, mostly in November during tryouts. When I was a young coach, I made a good friendship with a very successful coach at a rival school. At that point, he had spent twenty years coaching basketball. He told me a master's thesis written by a basketball coach in California claimed that a high school basketball coach estranges about 10% of the population every year.

"I guess that means that in my twenty years," he said, "I've pissed off 200% of the population." I was a young coach at the time and just laughed, thinking he was joking. The next year, despite being an outstanding and very successful coach, he was canned.

After 23 years, I suppose I had accomplished the same feat. That was a part of the job that I didn't like. Much of the grief comes in November as a result of annual tryouts. In fact, to this day, the month of November comes around and I still get a bit anxious. Each year I had to cut 10-25 boys from our basketball program. Do the math and that makes between 230 and 575 boys cut from my program over the years. If you include their immediate families and relatives, the number of those slighted skyrockets. In a group of communities of fewer than 10,000 people – well, you see the carnage. To paint a more accurate picture though, most of the boys and their families were upset for a few weeks, got over it and went on with life. The communities where I coached are full of great people.

A school board is elected by the local constituency to represent them in the school system. Most of the board members who served during my tenure as coach were fine people trying to do their best to support the educational programs within their jurisdiction. Even so, three of the members of this board at the time were not fans of mine. They sent me to prison.

The superintendent did everything in his power to make my "sentence" as palatable as possible. Nonetheless, it was not negotiable, and it was a blow. I was going to "The Island of Misfit Toys." He assured me that the board members antagonistic to me would be voted out in next election cycle and that new board members would be elected. My stay in prison wouldn't be more than a year or two.

He was confident that if I were patient, I could get back into the public school system sooner rather than later. The high school faculty was supportive of me staying at the school, and created a petition stating their case. But rather than make a mess at the school and cause a turf war, I decided I would take the superintendent's direction and "do my time."

Still, I was devastated. What would I tell my family, my friends? My ego was crushed and my dreams shattered. I became an educator and coach to help young men navigate the sometimes confusing and wandering teenage years, not old men who didn't deserve my efforts. I was going to prison!

Having driven past the prison hundreds of times, seldom had I thought much about it and when I did, it was not positive. Like the large majority of our population, I considered those incarcerated as the dregs of society. They didn't deserve anything and needed to rot in jail. Now I was joining them. Since they had no value, I now had no value.

This was my thought process upon receiving my sentence.

Little did I know the adventure that awaited me. To skip quickly through the narrative, within a very short period of time, I came to realize the great need and great opportunity before me. We started to implement a plan that would effectively increase the enrollment of Central Utah Academy, the secondary school inside Central Utah Correctional Facility that I supervised, by four-fold.

I had no idea in 2011 when I received my sentence that the next eight years would be the most fulfilling and enjoyable years of my professional career. The academy went from being "The Island of Misfit Toys" to the largest school in our school district. It was not uncommon to have some of the very men who, some months prior had been in my office complaining that they had to come to school, stand in my office door way and tearfully thank me. It is important to realize that they were really thanking the dedicated faculty, staff and inmate tutors who spent so much time and energy helping and serving.

To emphasize this by recapping our successes, by the end of seven years we had 80% of the Gunnison prison inmates either enrolled in the prison academy, enrolled in a post-secondary program we started in our third year (UPrep), or working as volunteers in one of these programs. In the Spring of 2018, of the 1,800 or so inmates incarcerated in CUCF, 1,052 were enrolled in CUA, 272 were enrolled in UPrep, 48 were workers in CUA and 128 volunteered at least 20 hours per week in one of these programs. All in all, 1,378 were directly involved in one or more of our programs. That makes around 80% of the inmates incarcerated in CUCF directly involved in our Educational program.

As a side note, because of our success at CUA, the principal involved in sending me to prison stayed at the local high school for an additional eight years. When I retired from my position at the prison, he voluntarily took the position of principal at the CUA. In addition, the school board member who lead the charge against me, also applied for a position at CUA.

Life is full of ironies.

Chapter 3

An inmate's perspective

To give the reader understanding of an inmate's life, this is the first of several inmate accounts to illustrate their perspectives. The reader is cautioned that some inmate comments may seem self-serving. Some parts may be difficult to read. However, it is important to hear from those who are impacted the most by the Utah Department of Corrections.

This is the sentencing experience of inmate Edmond in his own words. He was instrumental in the creation of two Central Utah Academy (CUA) Educational programs described later.

My name is Edmond. I am forty-five years old. I am best known to the state of Utah by my offender number. I have currently served 10 years of an indeterminate life sentence with approximately two more years of prison to go before I am required to complete a three-year parole. I was sentenced to prison for two acts of domestic violence committed against my now former wife in the summer of 2009.

I originally pled guilty to four charges: 1st degree aggravated burglary, 2nd degree attempted aggravated assault, 2nd degree aggravated assault, and 3rd degree domestic violence in the presence of a child. In the State of Utah, most 1st degree felonies carry a 5-years to life sentence while 2nd degree felonies carry a 1-15 years sentence and 3rd degree felonies carry a 0-5 years sentence. All sentencing to prison is indeterminate and left to the Utah Board of Pardons and Parole (BOPP) and their unfettered discretion.

Thus, actual sentencing is determined only after an offender is sent to prison and seen by the BOPP. This means an offender has no real idea about what kind of time he or she will potentially have to serve in prison from their first court sentencing.

By design, this method of sentencing could be a useful tool to determine the sentencing needs of a single offender and actually use time reduction as a way to incentivize rehabilitation and reform. It could also be used to further incarcerate those offenders who do not choose rehabilitation for themselves. Unfortunately, however, the BOPP and the UDOC have failed to use this tool effectively. They are either unqualified and inept in rehabilitation, or they simply are abusing their power and misusing this tool. I would argue that both are true to some extent.

When I accepted the terms of a plea bargain and pled guilty to my charges, I was told by my legal defense attorney, a public defender, that I would likely have to serve between forty-eight and seventy-two months in prison. Finding that to be acceptable for what I had done to my wife, I agreed to plead guilty to the charges. It would be another three years after being sentenced to prison by the judge that I would be informed by the BOPP that my sentencing matrix suggested that I serve one hundred and one months for my crimes, not forty-eight to seventy-two as previously implied.

Entering prison

When I first fished in [entered the Draper prison], I went through Receiving and Orientation (R&O). This had three stages. The first was to assess my well-being. On the first day I was stripped of all my belongings and photographed from head to toe while standing naked. Over the course of the next week I saw the doctor, dentist, caseworker and had

15

to complete a Test of Adult Basic Education (TABE) for the Education department.

The medical technician (not a doctor) asked several simple questions: "Are you taking any medication?" "Do you have any allergies?" "Are you a threat to yourself or anyone else?" Etc. When I went to the dentist, he took x-rays of my teeth and did a quick check-up. I found out that prison dentists "don't do any preventative care." He said that, "we basically pull teeth and fit for dentures."

When I saw my caseworker, he gave me a miniature assessment. His job was to determine my case action plan (mapping). His question were personal questions about my marital status, number of kids, educational attainment, etc. That experience lasted no longer than 5 minutes. After that, they did a DNA swabbing and took a head shot for my prison ID. The last thing they gave me was an orientation packet with "the rules."

My first encounter with an officer happened on my 3rd night after getting there. One of the guys in my housing section was a singer who seemed to know the words to every song. As requests were made, he'd sing the lyrics out with beauty and ease. It was such a wonderful thing for myself and the other inmates. During the one-and-a-half years in county jail during my trial, I hadn't heard music. This was a very nice change.

Without any warning, the night sergeant and two other officers ordered us to strip down to our underwear and cuff up. The officers placed handcuffs on each of us and then escorted us individually down the main hallway to a large holding cell. They returned to our section and proceeded to tear up everything in our cells. To this day I'm perplexed about why this happened. Had we broken a rule? If so, nobody told us. The only reason I can think of was for intimidation/bullying purposes. Being paraded down that hallway in my underwear was completely humiliating.

After a couple weeks, I was transferred to another unit for the remainder of R&O. That was about a 6-week experience. The entire unit was on 23-hour-a-day lockdown. Inmates were allowed, four at a time, to be out of our cell for one hour a day. Needless to say, it was a race to the shower (there being only one).

At some point, the chaplain came to my cell and gave me a set of scriptures that I had requested. Towards the end of my six weeks in that unit I was seen by another caseworker. His job was to determine if I was fit for general population or if I would have to start out in Maximum Security as a level 2 inmate.

The assessment was already done when I got there. He handed me a pink carbon copy of my points and said I was a "Kappa," and after R&O, would be sent to general population. Each inmate is designated as a Kappa = aggressive (violent), Omega = assertive (non-violent) or Sigma = passive (sex offender). Then he asked me if I had any questions. Boy did I! I spent a half hour with him going over all my questions. I wanted to know my sentencing matrix, how long before I could see the BOPP, how to go about completing my mapping, how long before I would be in front of the BOPP, would I be transferred to CUCF, how would I get into a program, etc. He was patient but had very few answers. When I was escorted out of his office, the other inmates waiting to see this caseworker were very upset. Most inmates take five minutes; I took 30 at least.

One of the most horrific experiences I ever had in prison happened during this phase of R&O. For three consecutive nights I had to listen as a youngster was being raped in an adjacent cell by a man twice his age and twice his size. Each night he would beg his cellmate to leave him alone. He would put up a good fight but in the end, he was forced to succumb to the violence of his perpetrator. On the third morning he attempted suicide and was moved to another housing unit. I prayed to God for the boy. I also prayed that

17

I would make it through this experience unmolested because I know if someone tried to do that to me, I would kill them. Not a good thing.

I saw that youngster about a year later in a Programming class we had together. Everywhere he walked he did so with his head down staring at the ground. When he would speak, he would never raise is voice above a whisper. I knew the moment that I saw him again that he would never recover from the violence he had endured.

The final stage of R&O was held in yet another housing unit. This unit was extremely intimidating. It had four levels with open bars on the cell doors. Everybody was yelling out the bars. It literally reminded me of the prison movies like "The Shawshank Redemption." There were an endless number of fights. Gangbangers fought against their rivals for drugs and territory. Sex offenders were assaulted for their crimes. It was nothing short of complete chaos.

Fortunately for me, I knew one of the trustees and he got me a trustee job within a day or two. This changed my out-of-cell time from three hours a day to almost the entire day. The position came with other perks as I got my share of extra food trays and yard time. It was a great blessing.

During this phase, my resolve was immediately tested. As a trustee, I was required by the officers to follow all the rules; no fighting, no tattooing, no gang activity, no substance abuse, no passing contraband to other cells, etc. On the other side, you are required by the inmates to: never be alone with an officer, pass their street drugs and prescriptions, food commissary, weapons and anything else they wanted you to pass. I was stuck between these two opposing forces and had to learn very quickly how to navigate myself or risk being beat up or worse. It was a Catch-22. If I followed the officers, then I would be labeled a snitch, rat, punk, bitch, or lame. All of which could get me killed. On the other hand, if I followed the inmates' rules then I was labeled a convict, less than human, a behavior

18

problem that needed addressing which would lead to my levels being sanctioned or being sent to Max. For me the decision was easy. I would follow all the rules of the facility while making sure that I never gave the officers anything they could use against another inmate. I had to become Switzerland if I was going to survive.

About half way through this experience I was asked by another inmate to pass some of his prescriptions to another cell. When I told him that I don't pass drugs or contraband, but could get someone who didn't mind doing so for a price, he threatened to beat me to a bloody pulp. I told this to my friend who had another trustee go up to the guy's cell and inform him that if he tried laying a hand on me that he wouldn't receive any more of his food trays and that all the other trustees would beat him down so badly that his own mother wouldn't recognize him. The inmate conceded, and on the next day, on the way to the shower, he offered an apology.

The whole experience confused me. Here I was supposed to be changing my life around and learn how to communicate without the use of violence. However, unfortunately, violence was the only language most of these men understood. It was their method of protection both in prison and on the streets. I was going to have to figure out how to conduct myself without violence while being completely surrounded by it. In the beginning I wasn't sure how it would all turn out.

Chapter 4

My R&O (Receiving and Orientation)

*A man who carries a cat by the tail learns something he
can learn in no other way.*

Mark Twain

Now for my own experience: Every inmate, as he "fishes
in" is required to spend several months in Receiving and
Orientation (R&O). Here, as the name suggests, they are
onboarded into prison life. My R&O as a principal at the
prison academy consisted of a couple days working with the
previous principal and a three-hour Corrections training on
protocol with inmates. The two days with the previous
principal let me know that I was about to be bored out of my
gourd and the volunteer training said I was about to enter the
valley of the shadow of death, so beware. Neither was right
but neither was wrong either.

At the first faculty meeting we had a frank discussion on
how I had arrived in prison. It didn't take too long for all of
us to self-identify as being sent to "The Island of Misfit
Toys." How could life get any worse?

As described by my predecessor, I found myself busily
reading the newspaper, standing in the hallway as
inmate/students trudged by, and constantly trying to keep
myself busy. I had determined to do my time and get out as
soon as the opportunity was available. There were no
expectations related to my assignment either by the school
district or by Corrections. I did, however, have expectations
set forth by the Utah State Office of Education (USOE). In
a weird way I now had three bosses. One, the local school
district whose job it was to help and monitor local public

schools. Though they were fairly supportive, and on several occasions the superintendent went out of his way to help, except for financial accountability, they had little real interest in what we did. My second boss was the UDOC. They preferred I stay silent and out of the way. And finally, the USOE, who was well-meaning and comparatively enthusiastic, though sometimes ineffective in its administration, at least at the beginning. Thankfully the USOE leadership started providing quality-directed leadership as time went on.

In the first 11 years of my coaching career I had the assignment of coaching the school's boy's cross country program. We were very successful and though it wasn't my first love, I found it enjoyable. That experience was much different than being the boys' basketball coach. With basketball, everybody cared and wanted their say. With cross country, just the opposite was true. In fact, Joe Davis, one of my coach mentors, explained to me that, "The best thing about cross country is that nobody cares. But, the worst thing about cross country is that nobody cares." That exactly described my new job at the prison.

I have always been a very high energy, active person. Had I grown up in this generation, I would have been diagnosed with ADHD and a well-meaning teacher or two would have prescribed Ritalin. My parents handled it differently. In my youth, from the time I was 5 years old, I spent the summers on my grandpa's farm working from sun-up to sun-down and looking forward to the next day. I truly enjoyed those summers, as did my mother, who received a well-earned break from my adventurous and sometimes obnoxious nature.

Finding myself in prison and never having been one to sit around and do nothing, I soon started looking around. What I found astounded me. First, because this school had limited funding, our textbook supply was very lacking. Our newest textbook was published more than twelve years before. Most were more than twenty-five years old. Lacking funding, the prison academy used hand-me-downs from the local public schools, making do with leftovers. Lacking textbook options, teachers had little choice but to create their own curriculum. Most had put together packets of material, broken down into 8-week segments designed to provide content for their students. Though well meaning, the instructors created packets that were no more than a hodge-podge. Students could earn credit for completing a 25-page packet and circling some answers. Those packets were often on about a 5th grade level.

Prison Education is part of the statewide Adult Education program. As I started attending the statewide Adult Education meetings and working with other Adult Education Directors around the state, I soon found that the same processes, curriculum problems and funding issues existed everywhere. It wasn't limited to the prisons and jails. The programs in the various communities around the state and the street programs suffered from the same lack of resources.

I went around to the classrooms and tried to take in the teaching. Most of it was self-paced and packet-based. Very little of it looked like a traditional classroom; a teacher leading students in learning. Not that the teachers were inept. If fact, over time it became obvious that most were good teachers. They just lacked direction and motivation.

We have a corridor with 12 classrooms at the prison academy. Of particular note was the classroom of one of the history teachers. The first time I went in, I walked into a dark room. Lights were off and black paper covered the security lights. The majority of lighting came from computer screens, a projector showing a movie and light coming through the doorway from the hall.

"We're in a prison?" I asked myself as I walked in. Looking around the room, I could see some of the inmates working on learning "packets." A couple more inmates worked on a computer-generated learning tool. Several others were drawing plays for the teacher, who also served as the football coach for a local high school. Another was doing logo designs for the same purpose and a handful were watching a movie on the big screen. As I walked out my first thought was: "That's got to go."

Each of the teachers had one or more inmate tutors hired to help them with their classes. These inmates worked as classroom aides and were paid about 40 cents an hour. Many of the Education tutors at the time were not always on the up and up.

The next thing I noticed was the amount of human resources being wasted. Of the 1,500 men housed at the facility, just over 200 of them attended the prison academy in one capacity or another. These 1,500 men wandered around with nothing to do but get into trouble. It was astounding. How can anything productive be accomplished when most of these people's biggest concern is what was on the dinner menu and whether their commissary was going to arrive on time, or with whom they were to play cards, or ping pong, or, occasionally, video games?

Being productive is something that creates our identity and our value. There was no method to the madness.

Imagine a life where you had no identity and no value. Imagine a life where you had nothing of value to occupy your mind or your time. Imagine a life where the only productive thing you could be involved in was wrong and/or illegal. Imagine a life where another person dictated everything you did. You get up when you're told. You go to bed when you're told. You never even turn a knob to open a door; it is either popped open or slid open in front of you. With few exceptions, you don't decide what you are going to have for meals, where you are going to sleep or who you are going to share your space with. Though there are some exceptions, inmates have very little positive identity.

I don't mean to imply that Programming, Corrections' Educational wing, offered nothing of value. That wasn't the case at all. Rather, a couple of dozen Programming classes offered by Corrections, when taken seriously, had great value and provided opportunity for inmates. The problem is these were seldom taken seriously. Likewise, inmates have the opportunity to earn high school credit and high school diplomas. However, most inmates looked at these with disinterest and contempt.

Finally, part of my responsibility was to go to meetings, some with the Utah Department of Corrections (UDOC) and some with the Utah State Office of Education (USOE). The first such meeting I went to with Corrections was a pat-on-the-back session. Each member of the group took turns stating the accomplishments and successes of their programs. During this first meeting, it seemed that all these successful programs existed throughout Corrections.

These meetings with Corrections consisted of a roundtable in which we sat around a huge board table, some 20 or so of us, and expounded the success of the previous few months. I was amazed at all the success. The sheer number of lives changed in that meeting would soon empty the cells and put Corrections out of business! (That would be a good thing, by the way).

And then there was mine. I felt my program was extremely inadequate. However, after attending several of such meetings over the first year of my time "down," I started seeing though the smoke and behind the mirrors.

Another part of my orientation was getting to know the inmates. The principal I was replacing advised me to not find out what individual inmates had done to be incarcerated. He felt like that information would make it very difficult to perform the responsibilities of administration with objectivity. In spite of that advice, he showed me where I could readily access that information. In my mind, I agreed with his assessment and determined early on to avoid finding out their crimes. Occasionally curiosity would get the best of me and I would investigate. From time to time there would be the inmate who seemed like he didn't belong. I would get curious and look him up. There would be the guy covered in tattoos and again, my curiosity would get the best of me and I would take a look.

But the former principal was right, it messed with my head.

Though most of the time I could look past it, there were several incidences in which I couldn't. Before long, I removed my access to that information. Though I could still find out with a simple google search, I discontinued the practice of looking.

I would like to share an example of finding out information about an inmate that illustrates the point.

Duncan, a teacher tutor, worked down the hall from my office. Without exception, every time he walked by my office in the morning on the way to his classroom he would stop and offer a heartfelt greeting. He stood about 6'5" and likely weighed near 300 lbs. He had thick black hair and coke-bottle-bottom glasses. He worked for a kind and hard-working teacher, who thought Duncan did a good job. Duncan was outgoing and considerate. He never spoke condescendingly to students and was humble and helpful. That daily greeting went on for about 5 months. I got to the point that I looked forward to him stopping by.

One evening at home in January, I was flipping through the channels on my TV and came across a documentary about a crime committed in rural Utah. The program was "20-20." I set down the remote and started to watch. Before long, the names of the two assailants were flashed on the screens with their mugshots. One of them was Duncan. Now I was hooked. For the next 30 minutes I found out in much more detail than I ever wanted to know about what he did to be incarcerated. I will save you some of the gruesome details, but they committed a horrific crime and murdered two innocent people.

I was horrified. I didn't sleep much that night. When I arrived at work and Duncan stopped by for his daily greeting, I couldn't look him in the eye. About three weeks later, I asked him to find a new job. I couldn't get past it. How could a guy that seemed so nice and considerate and gentle have committed such gruesome acts?

Another story actually comes from a different angle and illustrates the other side of the pendulum. My first year there, I decided that I wanted to teach a class so that I could get a feel for the teaching process. I was an algebra teacher through most of my high school career and so I determined to offer a math class. Part of being a teacher at CUA was having one or more tutors. There were always inmates who wanted to be tutors and their services were nearly always valued.

It was the spring of my first year when an inmate named Reggie approached me looking for a job. He seemed nice enough so I asked him to come to class and we would see how it worked out. As it turned out, we had a lot in common. We both loved basketball and had played into Junior College. We both graduated high school around 1980, me a little before and him a little after, and had many of the same likes. He had only been in prison about a year and I think I provided a safe place for him. Like him, I was still in my first year and I came to enjoy his friendship.

One day he walked into my office and asked me if I knew why he was in prison. I quickly responded that I didn't know and didn't care to know. I found it odd that he persisted in the conversation and wanted to tell me his story. In spite of my continued objection – having just fired Duncan – he continued.

As he told his story the whole thing became clear. It was a story with which I was very familiar. Several years prior, in the fall, there had been a rather notorious shooting in the state. As Reggie related his story, I remembered watching the whole thing on the evening news. His daughter had come home late at night frantic that a man in a black Chevy Tahoe had been following her and chasing her for the third night that week. Upset, Reggie had grabbed his 45-caliber pistol, and, with his daughter in tow, headed out the door. After a short drive, they found the Tahoe. Reggie sped around and cut it off. Getting out of his car, Reggie moved towards the other vehicle. The man in the Tahoe jumped out and chambered a bullet in his Glock. Without hesitation, they both fired. Reggie hit him twice in the stomach. Sounds like something out of the wild, wild West!

Anyway, the case went to court and Reggie was found guilty. I remember thinking at the time that he should get a medal rather than a sentence. What red-blooded American father wouldn't defend his daughter? Well, the prosecution made the "victim" out to be a saint. He was on neighborhood watch, they said. He was protecting the community, they said. Now he was in a wheelchair and this vigilante had ruined his life. At the time, I didn't believe the "victim's" story. Watching him in the courtroom, it was easy to see that he was not the saintly victim the prosecutor made him out to be. They had dressed him in a nice suit including a tie to make him look respectable but it was easy to see he was in no way a saint.

About six months after Reggie's conviction, the "victim" was on trial for multiple sexual assault charges among others. Come to find out, once in a wheelchair, three victims came forward explaining that they had been raped multiple times by the "victim" and he had used his collection of exotic snakes and his small arsenal of weapons to threaten them and their families if they ever told the police. They each explained that now that he was in a wheelchair, they knew he couldn't carry out his threats. Sadly, although these statements came forward during Reggie's trial, the judge would not allow them into evidence. Reggie was sentenced to 5 years to life and sent to prison.

Reggie continued to fight the charges claiming justifiable self-defense. It took another four years before he gained his release. He continued to work in Education for much of that time.

Reggie's story was a very rare case. In fact, it is the only case I am aware of where the inmate "didn't do it." Though I suppose he did.

Reggie, though technically a criminal, became a good friend and continued to work for me off and on for the next few years. Upon his release from prison, we became golfing buddies and still communicate regularly. His wife and family are very grateful to have that part of his life behind them. In Reggie's case, ignorance wasn't bliss. It helped me a great deal to know the circumstances of his incarceration.

Needless to say, I was well assimilated into my version of prison life.

Chapter 5

Recidivism: The Measurement of Failure

So many days where we talked ourselves hoarse,
believing we were touching each other's souls.
Hans Christian Anderson
"The Emperor's New Clothes"

Recidivism – the tendency of a convicted criminal to reoffend.

The buzzword in the Corrections system is RECIDIVISM, a word I had never before heard. It seemed that everywhere I turned, someone repeated the magic word. Reducing recidivism seemed to be at the top of the list of priorities within the UDOC and within Programming, the education arm of Corrections.

The first fall I went to a quarterly meeting in which all the groups that were responsible for Programming met to discuss their successes in reducing recidivism. We met in a board room in south Salt Lake. Being the new kid on the block, I had no idea what to expect. In the short period of time (about three months) in my new position, all I had seen was poor effort and few results. I thought we would come together to strategize how to improve the system and processes. That was not the case.

The Director of Programming for the UDOC took charge and started the meeting off by patting everyone on the back for their great efforts and strong desire to help. The subsequent activity was to go around the table one by one and state the great successes and outcomes from the previous year and how we were all making great strides to reduce recidivism.

It was impressive to spend over an hour listening to all the great achievements of the various Programming departments of the Corrections system. No less than twenty people spoke of their individual programs and touted their outcomes and successes. I was impressed. The principal of South Park, the school in the prison in Draper Utah, spoke for five minutes touting the accomplishments of his program. As I recall they had over 200 graduates the previous year and had given an amazing number of credits to their students. They had over 1,000 students and seemed to have a strong impact in all aspects of the prison in Draper.

When my turn came, I had little to say that was positive about CUA. From my perspective we had little to boast about. I remember thinking that I had a lot of work to do and better get a move on.

I had heard the word recidivism many other times in the previous 3 months but had no idea what it meant. I didn't want people to think that I wasn't knowledgeable about such an important word. At first I wondered if it was an acronym, something Corrections is extremely famous for. In this meeting I heard it over and over again and came to think that all these people were doing a great job in reducing the number of men that return to prison. I heard the idea that recidivism in the state was at about 30%. That sounded pretty successful to me. If only 30% of felons released on parole returned to prison, I would say the system was working. The problem is, as I came to find out upon returning to my office and asking Google, the recidivism rate in Utah and across the nation was closer to 70%. Thirty percent get out and stay out. I suppose that they used 30% in the meeting because it sounds so much better. Or, maybe I just misunderstood.

Upon returning to my office and finding out the truth about recidivism, what it meant and what the real numbers were, I began to see through the smoke screen. The scene wasn't pretty. The efforts and outcomes described in that meeting may or may not have been accurate. I had witnessed first-hand a dog and pony show. All fluff and no substance. Like it or not, little or nothing was being done to change behavior. According to a study done by the Rand Corporation, 33% of inmates released on parole will make the change not to return without any intervention. From the perspective of that data, the UDOC was having no positive effect.

I spent twenty-three years coaching boys' basketball in high schools. During those years, we met our share of success. We had great boys who worked hard and sacrificed and succeeded. I had one season where we only won five games. That equates to winning 32% of our games. I was nearly run out of town on a rail. How could a 30% success rate concerning men's lives be acceptable?

For the next few weeks, I read everything I could get my hands on related to reducing recidivism. There were studies done in the Florida Corrections system. There were studies done in Louisiana and Washington State. They all said the same types of things and gave the same basic statistics. The one I felt to be most accurate, however, was done by the Rand Corporation, "Evaluating the Effectiveness of Correctional Education." It is an 80-page document and goes into great detail on what actually works when it comes to reducing recidivism. We have used it as our Bible as we have implemented and evolved our programs.

To sum up its findings, The Rand Corporation found that, "...on average, inmates who participated in ... Education programs had 43 percent lower odds of recidivating than inmates who did not." According to their findings, the Education programs referred to were not crime-related rehabilitation. The Education programs emphasized by The Rand Corporation were secondary Education programs, vocational programs or postsecondary/college level programs.

The same study found similar positive outcomes when it came to post-incarceration employment. Inmates who

31

successfully completed prison Education programs were employed at a rate "...13 percent higher than ... those who had not participated." Vocational training resulted in the largest percentage of improvement in the area of employment. They found that "...individuals who participated in vocational training programs had odds of obtaining post-release employment that were 28 percent higher than individuals who had not participated." http://www.rand.org/jie/projects/Correctional-education.html.

At about the same time I found the UDOC Mission Statement which reads:

> *Our dedicated team of professionals ensures public safety by effectively managing offenders while maintaining close collaboration with partner agencies and the community. **Our team is devoted to providing maximum opportunities for offenders to make lasting changes through accountability, treatment, education, and positive reinforcement** within a safe environment.*

We had found our purpose and path. According to The Rand Corporation and the UDOC Mission Statement, Education was not to be cast aside. We were vital to the true success of the UDOC.

It was about this time that Inmate Edmond and I started working very closely together as we built the CUA/Outreach program. I might note that he and other inmates did most of the heavy lifting. My job was to approve processes and procedures and clear the path.

Chapter 6

Prison Education

Education is learning what you didn't even know you didn't know.

Walt Disney

I realized that I needed to learn about something that I knew very little about – education inside a prison.

One of the meetings I attended was the weekly Management Review (OMR), meetings held for each housing unit. There, we were supposed to discuss specific needs of specific individuals housed in that unit. I found the meetings … typical. I would go in and the staff was considerate and cordial. However, I felt like a bit of a sideshow. Maybe I misread their intention but I didn't feel like much of an asset.

I determined that I was going to spend time in each unit, especially with the captains and caseworkers. As that process continued over time, I found myself in the Gale Housing Unit. This unit was very different from the other units in the prison. Where all the other units had three separate sections with multiple cells that housed two inmates each, Gale was set up as a dorm, more like an army barracks. Here there are six separate sections with no cells. Each section had four "pods" with a couple dozen or so beds in each. Each inmate had a "Bunkie" and his own individual space. Their "cell" included two beds and a modified desk but no doors and only half walls outlining a space that could be compared to a cell. It was an interesting arrangement, very different than anything else in the facility. As I would come to find out, some inmates really liked it and others really didn't.

After a short time, I came to realize another big difference. The captain, officers and caseworkers in the Gale housing unit had a much different approach to their responsibilities than most officers in other units. There was a different feel. Gale functioned on production and incentives using a program they call STRIVE.

To be a part of the STRIVE program, inmates had to qualify and apply to come to the Gale Housing Unit. Once there, they had to live a specific code and meet specific requirements to remain. Like all units, they had inmate representatives for each section or pod. Like all units, inmates were given more "freedoms" based on their Permission Matrix Level (PML). However, unlike any other housing unit at CUCF at the time, inmates were required to have a 40-hour productive schedule each week and were held accountable for their activities. By completing their requirements, they could move up in their privileges. I saw there a system similar to the one regular people live in every day; be responsible, pay the price, get the reward. Over a very short period of time, Education and STRIVE formed a strong relationship that exists to this day. Many of the processes that we put in place in Education had genesis in STRIVE.

The 40-hour productive schedule could be any viable, credible activity. Gale inmates have the option to go to school, have a prison job, participate in STRIVE courses, volunteer in many different functions or be a part of the STRIVE leadership, etc. In essence, rather than sit around and get into trouble, the favorite pastime of many inmates, they got out and produced. As they did so, they were given opportunity to progress up through the system and receive more and more incentives. They had options through their good behavior to purchase better pillows, better mattresses, video games, TV privileges and the like. Like life in the real world, as they performed and produced, they were given more opportunity and more reward. They were given choices and when they chose correctly, they were incentivized and rewarded for them. They were incentivized to stay productive much as regular people are. Much of the incentive was the simple fact of getting out of the typical prison politics and being in a civil, "normal" environment. From where I sit, Gale is the most productive housing unit in the entire system.

As a side note, four weeks before I retired, I was visiting with the captain of the Gale housing unit. He told me that the recidivism rate for inmates housed in Gale who participated in the STRIVE program was 10%!!!

Yet despite their success, like our revamped Education program, Gale and STRIVE are in a constant battle with Corrections administration to keep their program. I have to ask why are STRIVE and the re-vamped Education always in a constant battle to be accepted by the UDOC? Both systems should be supported and replicated.

I quickly realized that I wanted to model our Education program in the same way. We set out to incentivize production and encourage compliance through positive rewards. The challenge then was to find a way to do this prison-wide.

The next thing I had to learn was how the prison system worked from an inmate perspective. The obvious best source for that information was all around me. In my short stay, I had made acquaintance with many different inmates. We had about twenty inmate workers we referred to as tutors that I dealt with in a regular basis. Among them, there was one in particular who I invited in to teach me.

Edmond, (whose experience is given throughout this book) had graduated from CUA the year before. In fact, he spoke at the graduation ceremony, as a student speaker selected by the faculty. Edmond was short and stocky and had a bit of a chip on his shoulder. He was also extremely intelligent, incredibly organized and was a very high-energy person. On the outside, he had, among other things, owned a construction business that built and remodeled homes on the East Bench of Salt Lake City. He had been very successful, which was a major factor that led to his incarceration. His was a rag-to-riches to dysfunctional to prison story that he'll tell you more of later. As for now, I saw Edmond as someone who could teach me the way inmates think and give me insight into their world so as to find a way to encourage them to become active participants in Education. He saw me as someone who had a real desire to do something different than the status quo. He soon became a valuable and trusted partner and friend.

We met daily, sometimes for hours. Often, we would invite other inmates into the conversation. My faculty thought I was crazy. The two principals before me had not been so engaged with inmates and had left well enough alone. They were more of a status quo kind of personality. That didn't work for me.

From Edmond I learned that one of the requirements set out by the prison but never enforced was that, to work in the prison, an inmate had to have high Test of Adult Basic Education (TABE) scores. This is the standardized testing the prison academy (CUA) used to evaluate individual academic achievement. A TABE test can be equated to any standardized test given in public education. It made an attempt to evaluate student levels and progress.

To work in the housing unit, inmates must score above 6, or Sixth Grade. To work a job away from their housing unit, all three of their TABE scores had to be above 9, or Ninth Grade.

At the beginning of my tenure, mentioning a TABE test to the average inmate created feelings of temper, and even anger. Eight years ago, inmates hated them, considering them to be just another stupid hoop they had to jump through. Within the first year that changed dramatically. The inmates now would cooperatively stand in line for their turn to test. Many requested it.

To illustrate the change in perception and attitude within the inmate population that occurred regarding the TABE testing requirement, let me relate a quick experience.

During the first Autumn of my eight years "down," in our efforts to figure out ways to recruit new students, we decided to take our product to them. I had been told stories of a principal 10 years prior who went out the various housing units to meet with inmates. I determined to take a similar approach. The school counselor and I set out to TABE test all possible candidates. I had the crazy idea to take the tests "on the road." With Anthony in tow, we made arrangements to gather groups of inmates in the various OMR rooms in each housing unit to test. On the first attempt, we found ourselves in a small room that was packed to the brim. There must have been 40 inmates in a room that could accommodate 30. The mood was borderline hostile. I started explaining our purpose and the discontent became obvious.

Looking around, there were no officers, only us two educators. We got a bit nervous. Not to be deterred, we continued the process, and in about two hours we completed our first group testing session. Though we managed to make it out alive, it was not a positive experience. We ventured to a second housing unit that afternoon and had a very similar experience. Enough of that: time to take a different course.

At that time, the average TABE score of inmates participating in Education was 5.3, just above 5th grade. Some were much higher and some were lower. Though education was needed by most and even sometimes required by court mandate, few participated. Initially, I thought that perhaps the inmates didn't care and wanted to do nothing and be nothing. However, I found that to be erroneous. In fact, just the opposite was the case.

The thing I most gleaned from my conversations with Edmond was that inmates were hungry for help. Though some had no interest in changing their behavior, many others had a strong desire, if given any opportunity, to pursue that opportunity and find ways to change their stars. When I realized that most of these men wanted to change, I wanted to provide that opportunity.

Under the current system, positive change is a nearly impossible uphill battle. Positive change is difficult for all of us. Adding the obstacles of a broken prison system makes it nearly impossible. But most often an inmate's desire is to improve and, if given the chance, he will move in that direction. After eight years in prison Education, working alongside many of them, I know this to be the case.

The question is, how could we get them to recognize the need to learn things they didn't even know they didn't know? How could we change the motivations towards and the opinions about Education at CUCF?

Chapter 7

The Beginnings

A journey of a thousand miles begins with a single step.
Ancient Chinese Proverb

The entirety of this chapter of the book is another narrative of Inmate Edmond. He gives a solid explanation of the beginnings of the prison academy's Outreach program. I might note that Edmond is one of the most dedicated, thoughtful, focused individuals I've ever met. As you read through this, you will understand how we were able to initiate such a breakthrough program, all the time fighting the culture of the UDOC:

After graduating from CUA, I began volunteering as an education tutor. Working with the new CUA principal, we started developing a curriculum that could be taught by an inmate to other inmates. We started with basic math and grammar. Three of us (inmates) worked on the project and got the courses approved for the STRIVE program in the Gale housing unit. Just as this was happening, I got moved to the Fir Housing Unit to start HOPE, a drug rehab program. During my intensive experience, I spent from 5 a.m. to 7 p.m. every weekday and then most of the weekends working on curriculum. Having successfully started "Outreach" in STRIVE, it made sense to enlarge the pilot program to include Fir.

I proposed the idea of expanding Outreach into Fir to the principal and he was immediately on board. He sent me to take the idea to the Fir weekly Management Review meeting (OMR). Having been there before and having had some success with my other requests, I was hopeful. Much to my chagrin, it was immediately shut down by the program director. He refused to entertain the idea. He wouldn't even let me get through the presentation. He saw it as a direct conflict to his beloved HOPE. Not one to take no for an answer, I went back every week for six weeks. Each week they would present problems that could arise. Each week I returned with solutions. After the sixth week I could see I was getting nowhere. Finally, I met with the principal and ask if he would go pitch the idea to Fir OMR. He asked me why I thought he would get a different response. My answer was simple. It's a whole lot easier to tell an inmate no than the academy principal.

The next day we went to OMR and presented the idea again. He went in and I stayed in the hallway with the door shut. It only took Mark about 10 minutes to convince them. At that point, he called me in and introduced me as the person who would work out all the details. I spent the next 10 minutes or so explaining how the program would run, when and where we would hold classes and who would be eligible. Mark ensured them that I would make sure everything was on the up and up and that he would follow up to ensure this was the case. They literally sat there, eating it all up like they were hearing all this for the first time. The program, CUA/Outreach, officially started in STRIVE, was now part of HOPE.

Over the next eight months I would often get called into OMR. As the program grew from initially having 3 students per class to averaging 25 students per class, their suspicions increased and the scrutiny became unwavering. I took it upon myself to write policy and procedure for the entire program. Those process we created, though evolved over time, remain at the base of all the CUA/Outreach programs throughout the prison (CUCF).

Despite my willingness to work hand-in-hand with security staff and resolve potential issues before they materialized, I was intensely harassed. Most of the officers surmised that my only reason for working so hard was because I was receiving some sort of ill-gotten gain. They would cancel our classes without notice. They harassed the students. They would treat me with utter disrespect. Two or three times a week they would "toss my cell" (tear it to pieces looking for contraband).

I would come home from Education where I worked and spent most my time to find all my belongings in a heaping pile in the middle of the floor of my cell. It was extremely frustrating. However, I kept my cool and learned to "kill them with kindness." It took nearly two years of these same events over and over before they realized that I wasn't going away. They finally started to work with me instead of against me. It only took two years.

The problems among the teachers of CUA were similar. When we started this project, there were just over 200 students enrolled in CUA. There were 12 faculty members. As you can imagine, the Education corridor was mostly empty most of the time. Starting Outreach posed a serious threat. They were sure that Outreach classes would be much easier than their classes, thus the students would flock to Outreach. They were sure we would help them cheat. The principal had his hands full trying to convince them that the glass was only half full.

To ensure the effectiveness of Outreach, we required every student to pass a post-test on the subject in order to receive credit. We created a testing center in the Education corridor. Every Outreach student was required to go to the center at the end of their course and take a final. Pass and they would receive credit. No pass, no credit. At the time, the curriculum for these or any of the other classes at the academy was very lacking. Most of the teachers used "packets" to teach their class. These packets consisted of 30-50 pages of 5th grade material worth a credit. As we developed Outreach, we created our own "textbooks." They were basically workbooks in which, as a student worked

41

through them, would learn the material while completing answers. At the end was a test they had to take in the testing center. They had to pass. It wasn't complicated but it was effective. The outcomes speak for themselves. From the onset, Outreach had a very high success rate.

Slowly the teachers witnessed the improvement of students and watched their class sizes grow. The enrollment of the academy doubled over the next six months, not only from Outreach classes but from interest in general. More and more inmates were enrolling – not only in Outreach but in teacher classes as well. The teachers also witnessed the improvement of students. The interest in the academy was growing. Teachers found hope in their jobs. We all began working for the betterment of students. It was "educational."

On the other side of the fence, I was getting harassed by the inmates. In their minds, since I had so much autonomy, I must be a snitch. Since I was unwilling to let them cheat, I must be a bitch. They were relentless in their attempts to get me to buckle. I was verbally attacked every day. Instead of collapsing to the pressure, I stood my ground. My answer was simple. "If you want to remain stupid then call me what you want, but if you want to learn what you don't even know that you don't know, then let me help you. I respect you way too much to just give you the answers." Anyone serious about improving their literacy levels put their trust in me and received an education. After a couple of years, I couldn't walk the halls without someone stopping me and with tears in his eyes thanking me for helping him change his life.

In the first two years we had increased the literacy levels throughout the entire prison. All our work was performance based. If it got results, we kept it. If it didn't get results, we tried something different. Every week the principal and I met, often for hours. We would go over the day-to-day operation of Outreach. Time and again we would run into roadblocks. Anytime we would run into a problem that seemed impossible to solve, he would turn to me and say, "Don't worry, have faith, the solution always presents itself." Never in my life did I have a person treat me with such love and respect. He trusted me implicitly and in return I gave him my all.

Our success grew and grew. We initialized a student database that could track the progress of every student. That data base was key in communicating with the housing unit caseworkers. We created a curriculum of 48 titles spanning as much of the secondary education subjects as we could. We worked very hard to match each with the state core curriculum. In the process of all that, we created our own printing operation. We had between 15 and 20 inmate workers who did research and developed curriculum, processed and formulated that curriculum into books and finally printed them. The process is like nothing you will ever find in any prison anywhere.

Our success spilled over into the other housing units. We engaged housing unit leadership to "recruit" our students. The database allowed them to see who was involved and who wasn't by simply opening the program we created, called Inmate Summary (SIS), on their computer. Inmates who needed education and were not enrolled were easily identified and sent to Education to get things going. Education became a requirement to advancing one's Permission Matrix Level (PML). We went from 200 to 400 students in the first year or so. Education, for anyone with low literacy levels, was now prison-wide. Within four years we had reached 800 students and climbing. Our student body involved over half the inmates at Gunnison (CUCF). We had started a new way of thinking. We were changing the culture of CUCF, at least in part.

Chapter **8**

The Workforce

...To thine own self be true.
William Shakespeare – Hamlet

One of the major problems we encountered early on had to do with the inmate help. After a short period of time, it became obvious that a good portion of the inmate tutors in Education had nefarious intentions. Much later on, after we "cleaned house," I had several of the inmate tutors tell me stories of tutors hiding stuff in the ceiling tiles for later retrieval, the inappropriate procurement of card stock or pencils or markers or paperclips. They took these items back to the house to use for barter. Even in prison, capitalism is king. Some tutors would run their store right out of Education. Inmates would come to the Education corridor, get their "stuff" and smuggle it out themselves. Sometimes they would bring their barter to Education and trade there. Other times it would be smuggled out and traded later.

Some former tutors would use their position to pass on messages between inmates and still others that would do their gang business from their tutor position. These activities by inmate tutors were not isolated to Education. Inmate workers in other areas of the prison still practice some of these inappropriate behaviors.

I knew that if we were to have a respected program, we had to eliminate the criminal activity amongst the inmate tutors.

We determined that we would hold a meeting and set down the expectations. From that meeting came the basic speech that I repeated every time we hired a new tutor and every time we had a tutor meeting, which was monthly for the next almost eight years.

As they entered the classroom, I greeted most of them by name and told them I appreciated any positive service they had thus far given to Education. I told them that Education does not hire criminals and that any kind of illegal activity would end at that moment. I really didn't know who was doing what. I just knew it was going on. So, the first thing I did was call them out as a group for their selfish activities. I wanted them to realize they were now working for someone who took notice and wanted to fulfill our responsibilities as a partner with Corrections. I wanted them to realize that growth and change were hard work but well worth it and that every person on the planet had the responsibility to roll up their sleeves and go to work improving themselves. I wanted them to realize they were responsible for their behavior and actions and that the consequences of their actions were a product of their lives lived, good or bad.

We discussed service and I told them that, "God doesn't care who you serve, He cares that you serve and that serving makes us human.

"The people we serve may or may not take advantage of what we do for them, but we will grow and become better people no matter how the service is received."

Some 25 years earlier, I was attending a coaching symposium at the University of Utah where Morgan Wooten spoke, the coach of what was arguably the most successful high school basketball program in America. At that event, he shared with us a poem that I shared with many of the players on my teams over the years. I determined to share it with these tutors. It was written by Peter Dale Wimbrow.

The Man in the Glass

When you get what you want in your struggle for self
And the world makes you king for a day
Just go to the mirror and look at yourself
And see what that man has to say.

For it isn't your father, or mother, or wife
Whose judgment upon you must pass
The fellow whose verdict counts most in your life
Is the one staring back from the glass.

He's the fellow to please – never mind all the rest
For he's with you, clear to the end
And you've passed your most difficult, dangerous test
If the man in the glass is your friend.

You may fool the whole world down the pathway of years
And get pats on the back as you pass
But your final reward will be heartache and tears
If you've cheated the man in the glass.

On first reading, this poem may seem selfish. However, upon further reflection, both this poem and Shakespeare's quote above are about being and becoming your best self with the consequence of making the world a better place.

Over a period of several years, many of the tutors in that first group said how that poem gave them a great deal of purpose and focus.

In that first meeting with prospective tutors, we talked about why they were in prison and what their futures might hold. We talked about purpose and direction, responsibility and accountability. I told them that I don't hire criminals and that if that's what they wanted – to continue in dishonorable ways – they should find other employment.

When we were done, I realized that it was a similar speech that I had given over and over again with the basketball teams I had coached. I came to realize that the path to success is pretty much the same for everybody. Having hope, purpose, direction, accountability, opportunity, getting over yourself, and serving others are the framework to a successful life.

From that first meeting came a core of five tutors who remained intact for the first five years of my time at the academy. One actually was still employed until six months before my retirement. All five continued to work for me in Education until they either paroled or were rolled up in the Inmate Placement Program (IPP) and sent to a county jail.

I gave the same speech to every new hire and each knew I was serious. That first year I had to fire half my tutor staff. Over time, the inmates realized that we were serious and that if they didn't want to join us and become part of our success, they could get off the train. To this day we have a loyal, committed, selfless tutor staff of some 45 strong that commit 40-50 hours per week, sometimes more, to help our Education program. They are far and away some of the best employees I've ever worked with. They are dedicated, responsible, accountable, self-directed, selfless and group-oriented. They bought into our philosophy and work endlessly to provide opportunity for others. I could leave work on Thursday and come back on Monday and find huge amounts of important tasks accomplished. It was truly amazing.

Chapter 9

Corrections, the Perfect Parent

*Children are natural mimics who act like their parents,
despite every effort to teach them good manners.*
Mark Twain

During my years working in public high schools, my
assignments ranged from coaching boys' basketball for 23
of those years to being the athletic director to teaching topics
from remedial math to Algebra II. During that time, I found
many great experiences working with students, athletes,
teachers, administrators, and parents. Possibly the most
complicated part of the puzzle was the parent piece. Most
parents were great and supported their kids and the school.
A few supported the school first and then their kids. But
others supported their kids blindly and the school not at all.
Here is an example to illustrates the point.

One of the many challenges in public school is appropriate
student dress. I was a freshman in high school when our
school went from slacks and button-up shirts for the boys
and skirts or dress slacks for the girls, (yes, I'm old) to jeans
and T-shirts. The new dress code was **great**, at least for most
the kids. Mix in the allowance of hair grown past the collar
or over the eyes for the boys and we thought we were in
heaven. The teachers had a hard time with it and most of the
parents didn't like it. However, once started, there was no
going back. That is likely what they feared.

Fast-forward 25 years. Walking down the hall of an
average high school in Utah in 2001, it is not uncommon to
see many well-groomed, modestly dressed kids. With that,
however, is the girl with the short skirt, the kid wearing the
wife beater, the girl with an obscene message on her T-shirt
and another kid saggin' (plumbers crack). The dress code of

the time, though liberal by most people's standards, did not allow any of those things.

As a teacher or administrator, dealing with those items was difficult, not because of the kids, but because of the parents. As a male teacher, addressing the concern of a girl's short skirt instantly made me a pervert. I'll never forget a call I had to make about a girl whose fanny was hardly covered. After a brief introduction, I addressed the daughter's dress code issue with the mom, who immediately responded, "What are you doing looking at (my daughter's) ass?" "What are you? Some kind of pervert?"

Then there were the boys saggin'. I have no idea how they kept their pants from falling to their knees! Who in any civilized society wants to see some kid's underwear, or worse? I can't count the number of times that, after addressing such a problem with a student and then with a parent, I was accused of singling them out or being out of line. "He can wear his pants however he wants." At least I wasn't accused of being a pervert!

The dress code issue goes back to the idea of responsibility and rights. Sadly, responsibilities are ignored and rights are screamed.

The problem is that the majority of students and parents of students didn't want to be subjected to seeing the kid's backside hanging out while walking down the hall or sitting in the classroom. What person wants their teenage daughter exposed to that? Back in the day it was considered voyeurism. Now, with parents having opposing views concerning appropriate dress and conduct, dealing with these and the myriad of other issues related to student conduct is a nightmare for teachers and administrators. Though some parents are supportive, the days of all parents getting behind the school's discipline and rules has passed.

Enter Corrections, the perfect parent. We affectionately referred to the captain of each housing unit as the dad and the caseworkers as the mom. In the early days of my time when we first started implementing the prison-wide policy of mandatory Education attendance for underachieving inmates, it was not uncommon to have guys in my office complaining about having to come to school. Many wanted to be exempted from the requirement. They would often list all the reasons that they couldn't come or shouldn't have to come to school. Most of the time, as long as they were civil, I would listen politely and offer insight and counsel along the way. I would talk about the UDOC mission statement which makes claim to partner with other agencies to provide opportunity for inmate growth and change. Then I would break out the Rand Corporation's "Evaluating the Effectiveness of Correctional Education," a study on effective recidivism reduction methods. I would simply tell them that as an educator, I could only exempt those who were intellectually challenged; the guys that really struggle, and since they didn't fit in that category, I could not exempt them from Education. However, their housing unit captain, (dad) had that authority and taking up their plight with him would be the way to go. I would dare say that none or nearly none of them went that route. You see, the one person in most housing units that an inmate did **not** want to see was the captain. In their mind, nothing good would come of it.

Word soon spread that though I was sympathetic and would listen to their concerns, the only way to get out of Education other than completing the requirements was through their housing unit captain (dad). The line of removal requests disappeared. In the early day I had two or three inmates a day making the request. After only several months, that number dropped to two or three inmates a month looking for an exemption and most of them were new to the facility.

Garnering the support of the housing units was not an easy task. Being the outlying program in the facility was not an easy thing for me. For most of my educational career, I was in the limelight. The boys' basketball program in most

50

schools in rural Utah is very important. It was not uncommon for us to play at home in front of a packed house and to take a large contingent of fans on the road. People cared about basketball. That was a two-edged sword for obvious reasons, but it meant that I was never cast aside as unimportant. That was not the case in this new position. In the beginning, Education was mostly considered a nuisance.

From hearing the stories of the past, I knew that some administrators took their assignment to heart and saw the need for a quality program but had marginal success. Corrections had "allowed" their existence because of legislative mandate. Educational programs are a requirement in the Correctional system but not viewed as valuable by Corrections, at least not judging from their actions. That was not gonna fly with us. We were able to identify an eager though reluctant student body, completely supportive yet apprehensive parents and a need to help people change their stars.

Garnering the support of the housing unit leaders would be critical to our success. And that proved to be the case. What started in the Gale Housing Unit soon spread to the other five general population units. A seventh unit, Ironwood, was built several years ago. They fell in line without a hitch. Finally, Hickory, a level 2 unit in which inmates are locked down most of the day because of either behavior or safety issues, started an Education program to help level 2 offenders move out of lockdown.

Because of the support of the officers in the housing unit, we had established a mandatory, incentivized, productive Education program. We have seen 400% growth in our student body. Thanks to their support, we have been able to start and effectively carry out additional incentive programs, such as Utah Preparatory Academy (UPrep) and Brickhouse [computer] Code Camp and other very valuable programs. We were starting to get the buy-in we needed to be successful.

Chapter 10

Moving into the 21st Century

To infinity and beyond!

Buzz Lightyear

We had to provide several important pieces of the puzzle to garner support from the housing units. They wanted to be supportive but claimed the volume of information about every inmate would overwhelm the system and that without accurate, up-to-date information, there would be no way to keep up. So, it was clear that in order to guarantee their support, we would have to find a way to provide inmate Education information to the housing units in an accurate and timely manner. That would eventually mean processing the information of about 1,500 men. We had to find a viable and effective way to provide accountability and follow up.

Up to that point, everything about Education in the prison was tracked by hand. It was virtually impossible to have any up-to-date information. A secretary painstakingly entered data every day on a spreadsheet that we provided to Corrections about our student/inmate's education. Needless to say, that information was months old. Very little of it was accurate. Nothing was automated. We had a state Student Information System (SIS) similar to most public schools but it was unavailable to Corrections staff. We had to figure a way to get up-to-date information to Corrections.

As the inmate council and I contemplated the problem, we determined to have someone write a software program that would be compatible with the state Student Information System.

Having no money to hire a computer programmer, we looked to the men in white. In a matter of days, an inmate named Michael appeared. Edmond introduced this older, balding man and suggested he could help us. Michael had been an engineer on a nuclear submarine in the navy. Having completed his tour, he retired and through a series of terrible decisions, ended up in prison.

Come to find out, he had an extensive knowledge of Excel, and claimed to be able to solve our SIS/communications problem with Corrections. Michael then set out to develop an amazing local SIS using only the Microsoft Excel spreadsheet. He had, within a very short time, using macros, created an efficient, comprehensive database that could use downloads from the state SIS databases combined with information from the Corrections database, and provide automated up-to-date information about every inmate in the facility to every captain, lieutenant, caseworker, etc.

The program was amazing. I'm sure that he could program and use Excel in ways that even the Excel engineers would not believe. With the click of a mouse, caseworkers could now check compliance with Education requirements for each individual inmate. They could now check if an inmate is eligible for a job. They could quickly check an inmate's schedule in Education and in Programming to ensure they are where they are supposed to be or identify where they are not supposed to be. This software provided quick and easy accountability of each inmate wherever he was.

We first introduced our "Inmate Summary" in the Gale Housing Unit. Our relationship with STRIVE ensured we could get the bugs out without being thrown under the bus. Within a short period of time, other units became interested in what we were doing and within a year of its inception, our "Inmate Summary" was implemented and used throughout the facility. Now, each inmate who had low TABE levels or had not graduated from high school was attending school. We had created a mandatory Education system. Over time, nearly every inmate who held down a prison job was

Education-compliant and eligible to have that job. Education had become an integral part of life at CUCF.

Through another inmate, Blaine, who had been a network engineer before coming to prison, we developed a way to easily deploy our information to all the CUCF stakeholders and viola, we had our database. For the next 3 years, until his parole, Michael upgraded and improved the spreadsheet that he had turned into a database. I can't count the number of times that I had him in my office asking if he could make a change or upgrade. He would sit in silence for several minutes staring into a far-off void and then suddenly, he would look at me and say, "I can do that."

We used that spreadsheet/database until about 2015 when we upgraded it to the language C++. That database has become a trusted part of the culture at CUCF. We have instant information as to the inmate's location, his Permission Matrix Level (PML), his caseworker, the classes he is enrolled in and the time he is enrolled, his Programming classes and their times, his TABE scores both past and present, and his graduation date or GED date. We even have a color-coded space indicating whether an inmate is eligible for a job. We have automated our book check-out system, which appears on the screen, and have a column for notes so that anytime we interact with the individual, we note it and can track his progress.

Caseworkers use our SIS system daily, as it is much easier than their own. It was interesting three years ago when we changed from the Excel version to the C++ version, the system was down for almost three weeks and my phone was ringing off the hook with inquiries from CUCF housing unit staff as to when the system would be back up.

That was a clear indication to me that we were no longer an expendable, marginal program, at least as far as the housing unit leaderships were concerned. They needed our SIS data to effectively manage their inmates. It was a good feeling. They needed us! We were an integral, valued part of the CUCF.

From there we created a system of identifying "education compliance." I don't want to go into the detail of the process. I'll simply say that the CUCF staff had all the information they needed to follow-up with each individual inmate and ensure education compliance. In a nutshell, more than 95% of inmates who have low test scores were enrolled and actively participating in our CUA program. Of those participants, progress is required and can be tracked by our SIS so that it is easy to identify any individual not in compliance.

One of the positive side effects of our SIS is that the housing unit staffs has great faith in our ability to come through. We work hard to support them in their efforts and they know that our information is correct and on time. To further support our processes, we have inmate liaisons assigned to every housing unit. These liaisons work with individual inmates as well as their caseworkers to help the inmate population in their units understand what is expected and remain education compliant. We also have a staff member who attends OMR every week in every housing unit to ensure good communication and follow through.

As a result of these and other measures, there has been a strong culture change towards education by some of the housing unit officers. They see us as a valuable asset rather than a nuisance. The bulk of the offenders who participate in education appreciate the positive way they are treated in Education. The self-fulfillment that comes from learning and growing intellectually changes their feelings of self-worth. The Education staff and tutors realize their desires to enrich the lives of their students. That internal change creates the outward changes.

This process has changed more lives than I can count. I'm not talking about complete turnarounds. We haven't solved the world's problems, not by a long shot. But we have helped so many men who failed miserably the first time they went through the Educational system. Imagine living your whole life not being able to read, then learning not only to read but to read on a 6th or 7th grade level or more. It is eye-opening. Imagine feeling hope for the first time in forever. Imagine thinking that perhaps there is a chance for growth and change and a better way of life. It is only the beginning.

If we could get someone in the upper echelons of Corrections and the state to catch the vision of our processes and how we are able to motivate inmates to improve, we could completely transform the prison system in Utah to be a true Corrections system. We could implement a tiered progress platform that would require inmates, of their own volition, to improve and get to the point that they are no longer fit for prison. They would be much better prepared to return to society a better person, ready to contribute and serve rather than take and victimize. (See the Chapter "A Real Solution") This may be nothing more than a pipe dream. But to me, for real change to happen, it is a must. Ironically, if done properly, there would be little additional upfront cost and immense savings as time passed and recidivism would be reduced. An inmate costs the State of Utah conservatively over $30,000 to house for a year. Reducing recidivism and thus the prison population by just 10% would reduce the annual cost to the taxpayer over $20,000,000. Just 10%.

Corrections is set up to be the perfect parent to change the lives of so many. What will it take to get those within Corrections to take notice and listen?

What will it take for the powers that be to realize that it is possible to create a system of self-selection that allows, encourages and supports individuals to move in a positive direction?

It would replace the current warehouse system that can be equated to a cesspool.

I believe the large majority of Corrections staff at CUCF agree with this idea. I have seen many of them make great efforts to provide such an environment. But, like many of the inmates, they, too, have lost hope.

In recent conversation with the Executive Director, I learned that finding new prison guards has become a nightmare and the parole system is completely overwhelmed. In addition, the new prison under construction west of the airport in Salt Lake City is two-thirds the size of the current prison in Draper. So many problems could be solved by making reduced recidivism an absolute priority rather than a buzz phrase. At some point, Corrections has to stop putting the cart before the horse.

Chapter 11

The Star Fish Parable

One day a man was walking along the beach, when he noticed a boy hurriedly picking up and gently throwing things into the ocean.
Approaching the boy, he asked, "Young man, what are you doing?"
The boy replied, "Throwing starfish back into the ocean. The surf is up and the tide is going out. If I don't throw them back, they'll die."
The man laughed to himself and said, "Don't you realize there are miles and miles of beach and hundreds of starfish? You can't make any difference!"
After listening politely, the boy bent down, picked up another starfish, and threw it into the surf. Then, smiling at the man, he said ...
"I made a difference to that one."

This painting was provided by an inmate who also wrote a personal narrative for this book. We used it as the front cover for the program of the 2019 graduation ceremony.

Another of the challenges I faced with my new assignment was one of apathy. The faculty and staff at the academy were good people wanting to do good things. However, like most of the other people who worked in the facility, they were stuck in a rut of low expectations and lack of focus.

The culture of the school was to give credits and get graduates. Whether they could read or write was not as important as graduations. The "rival" prison school, South Park, (the name of the prison school in the Draper Prison) had an even stronger culture in that regard. Credits were earned for doing a forty-page stapled packet of 5th grade material. Whether it was reading or math or language or science, "push-em through" was the philosophy.

I don't really blame the teachers. They were doing the best they could do in the situation they were put in. Sometimes it's hard to care when no one else does. Sometimes it's hard to persist when you're constantly fighting the system. The generally hopeless nature of the prison had rubbed off on the academy staff.

To have success, we needed motivation, purpose and hope. We had already started rolling out some of the ideas we had come up with in the inmate council as described in the previous chapter, "The Beginnings." We were starting to communicate directly with caseworkers, captains, sergeants, etc. to get some buy-in. It was slow, but in the Gale Housing Unit, things were moving. There we started a mandatory attendance policy. In a nutshell, all inmates housed in Gale were required according the STRIVE model to take the TABE test to assess their education levels. Any inmate scoring below the 11th grade was required to enroll in Education *and* show annual progress in their lowest functioning level, Reading, Language, or Math.   In addition, we started offering Education courses in the Gale housing unit.

Ironically, most of the faculty went into a panic. They said:

"Our classrooms will be empty."

"All the students will enroll in Outreach (the name of the new program) and won't enroll in our classes."

"The quality of instruction and learning will plummet."

"They won't need us anymore."

From my view, it was quite narrow-minded but that didn't change the fact that they were very concerned. All I could see were 1,500 individuals who needed education. At the time, we were providing service to about 12% of that population. There was lots of room to grow.

That first spring of my tenure we determined to create a new culture in the faculty and introduced the Starfish Story. We purchased mouse pads with the Starfish Story printed on it and gave each teacher a keychain with a starfish and a reminder of helping the one. This was not a new philosophy. It was just missing in the academy.

The faculty caught on very quickly. They soon came to realize that we had a unique opportunity to help a forgotten population. It was encouraging to see the results of their labors as they saw a new vision and purpose in their jobs. In a very short time, our student enrollment had doubled in size.

Though some of the teachers on staff had come to prison by choice, others had been propelled out of the public education system. They were unwanted. Like me, they themselves had been cast aside, placed somewhere where they would be out of sight and out of mind. As they started to explore our new approach, the light and interest in their responsibilities started to shine through. It was fun to see the new glow in their eyes as they came to work and the new purpose in their teaching.

The same transition was happening for the inmate tutors and even the students. More and more inmates found

Education to be an enjoyable place to be either as a student or a mentor. Here they were treated like normal people. Here they felt appreciated. Here they started to find hope. Here they either felt like the little boy throwing the starfish back into the sea or like the starfish, being thrown back to get a new lease on life.

The faculty that remained after my retirement had that vision. They are great people with a fantastic vision of prison education. They are willing to find methods that worked. They are willing to provide hope and opportunity.

To illustrate the change needed, consider the case of Jack Welch, CEO of General Electric.

"If the rate of change on the outside exceeds the rate of change on the inside,
the end is near," he said.

Jack Welch was named by *Fortune* magazine as the greatest CEO of all time. Though not well-known outside the world of big business, he "changed the rules of the game." As CEO of GE, he took the hundred-year-old stagnated conglomerate and transformed it into an up-and-coming growth business, something that was unheard of.

He was blowing up the bureaucracy, eliminating the formalized meetings that had long marked GE's culture, and installing a blunter, more freewheeling style that prioritized "facing realities" over "superficial congeniality," as Welch later put it in *Jack: Straight From the Gut*. He was beginning to execute on his famous dictum that if a GE business wasn't first or second in its market, it should be sold, fixed, or closed.

Jack changed the culture at GE. He changed the "inside" in order to change the "outside."

The outward growth of the prison academy was a result of the inward growth of our people, converting them from a state of "don't get it that they don't get it," to a state of getting it. The process requires that each individual "come to themselves." This process happened not just within our students but mostly within the people providing the new, valuable service.

That growth didn't come without a great deal of pain and work. The biggest change occurred with the attitudes of the housing unit leadership, of the prison academy faculty and staff, and of the inmates housed at the prison.

That first year, through the information I gained from the inmate council we formed, as well as information gained from the Gale housing unit from the Captain on down, we formulated a plan of action to encourage change on the inside so we could effect change on the outside.

The culture we have created is incredibly unique inside a prison. It is a culture that is evident in any quality organization. Stakeholders have hope in success. They all have a clear path to success and if followed, they are rewarded for that success. The process is one of self-selection and self-driven destiny. Success requires hope, opportunity, accountability, purpose and rewards for success, all of which create positive feelings of self-worth. There is no entitlement. No one in the program is allowed to wallow in the "I deserve this service" mentality.

Our students earn the right to participate in our post-high school UPrep program and do not want to lose that opportunity. Our UPrep participants are focused on their responsibilities and not on their rights. It works. I've seen it. It is not a new concept to the world at large but it is a new concept inside a prison.

Growth on the outside is always a result of growth on the inside.

The faculty likewise gained that vision. They are great people with a fantastic vision of prison Education. They are willing to find methods that work. They are willing to provide hope and opportunity. Listening to our students and inmate tutors, our faculty serves as a beacon of hope in a world of gloom.

Unfortunately, UDOC administration didn't have the same perception of our success. In talking with my former faculty since my retirement, UDOC administration is drastically changing Education. They are cutting back on the incentives and rewards we were providing and placing additional limits on Education's positive reach.

Chapter 12

People that don't get it
don't get that they don't get it

It was six men of Indostan,
To learning much inclined,
Who went to see the Elephant
(Though all of them were blind),
That each by observation
Might satisfy his mind.

The First approach'd the Elephant,
And happening to fall
Against his broad and sturdy side,
At once began to bawl:
"God bless me! but the Elephant
Is very like a wall!"

The Second, feeling of the tusk,
Cried, -"Ho! what have we here
So very round and smooth and sharp?
To me 'tis mighty clear,
This wonder of an Elephant
Is very like a spear!"

The Third approach'd the animal,
And happening to take
The squirming trunk within his hands,
Thus boldly up and spake:
"I see," -quoth he- "the Elephant

Is very like a snake!"

The Fourth reached out an eager hand,
And felt about the knee:
"What most this wondrous beast is like
Is mighty plain," -quoth he,-
"'Tis clear enough the Elephant
Is very like a tree!"

The Fifth, who chanced to touch the ear,
Said- "E'en the blindest man
Can tell what this resembles most;
Deny the fact who can,
This marvel of an Elephant
Is very like a fan!"

The Sixth no sooner had begun
About the beast to grope,
Then, seizing on the swinging tail
That fell within his scope,
"I see," -quoth he,- "the Elephant
Is very like a rope!"

And so these men of Indostan
Disputed loud and long,
Each in his own opinion
Exceeding stiff and strong,
Though each was partly in the right,
And all were in the wrong!

John Godfrey Saxe

People who don't get it don't get that they don't get it. Few other sayings or isms explain people's behavior better than

65

this statement. Mix that with the quote by Walt Disney, "Education is learning what you didn't even know you didn't know," and you have *the* biggest obstacles to change in the human family.

I wonder if the point at which one "comes to oneself" is simply when one learns to ask the right questions rather than give all the right answers.

A classic example of this idea came to me while spending many years teaching algebra to teenagers. Math is an interesting subject. There are those that get it and though it may sound hard to believe, for those people math is easy and it makes sense. For others, math does not come so easy. Though they may be good writers or good athletes or good artists, they may struggle identifying the concepts of math and putting it all together. I don't mean to imply that artists or writers or athletes cannot learn math. That is not the case. Some people are good at all those things and more, as well as math. But often, there seemed to be students who struggled understanding algebra yet succeeded well in other areas.

Math builds on itself. One concept and topic lead to another. In algebra, for example, through pre-algebra, algebra I and algebra II, even into college algebra, most of the basic topics are the same. They are just presented at a deeper level. It was not uncommon to have struggling students who, after muddling their way through factoring equations or some other concept would come up and suggest we go back a year because they "…got it then." They had a hard time seeing that, perhaps they did get it then, but it was at a lower, easier level. Going back and redoing the same thing would not constitute learning. It may constitute re-learning. Many of these students wanted to go back to when math was "easy." Thus, they saw many of their peers get it and in spite of all else, they couldn't come to grips with the reason they didn't get it was about them; not their peers, not the teacher, not the content.

Another possible example of people who don't get it and don't get that they don't get it is the basketball coaching world. I worked hard to prepare to become a coach. I will be the first to admit that, in the early days, I thought I knew it all. The thing is, I wasn't the only one. Many in the stands thought they knew it all, too. In my early coaching days, I was one of the people along with those many in the stands that didn't get that I didn't get it. Every game night I put my wares on display. Good or bad, we went to battle doing all we could to perform well and win. As time went on, even though I had a pretty darn good knowledge of basketball, I came to realize all that I did not know. That realization of learning to ask the right questions helped me to improve my abilities and become more successful. Without that understanding, I would have never stayed at it for 23 years nor would we had near the success.

As a rural town basketball coach, I was responsible to ensure that the junior level programs were successful also. Part of that process was finding coaches to lead the various teams from 3rd grade on up. Often the local community organizations took care of many of the details but I was often involved. I found it interesting to watch as some of the volunteer coaches came and asked for some direction and help while others did not. It was interesting to see the evolution over the years of many who, like me, came to realize that they didn't get it. I enjoyed helping them move from the world of people that "don't get that they don't get it" to a realization that there are a lot more questions than answers.

I found this to be the case as I have worked with Corrections personnel. Most of them were good people with good hearts and a desire to help. Like the faculty I encountered when I first came to CUA, the Corrections personnel were doing the best they knew.

Yet the bureaucracy is stifling and the inconsistency is shackling. The quarterly meetings described earlier (that

67

have now gone by the wayside) were a classic example of that. As we continued with the meetings, I tried to interject the idea that there was room for improvement or that perhaps if we looked from a different perspective, we could come up with ways to improve our outcomes. One time I even suggested that achieving a 70% recidivism rate was, according to a bell curve, going to happen no matter what efforts Corrections makes. I pointed out that statistically, 33% of incarcerated persons who were paroled would not return. That didn't go well. No one in that group wanted to take any ownership.

I'm grateful for police officers. They are critical members of society. They are in place to keep the peace, to keep people safe, to control the unsavory element. Working with them over these years I have come to appreciate how much most of them are concerned about society. They want to do the very best they can. They are to be commended. As with all professions and occupations, there are a few bad apples.

There is, however, a difference between the typical personality of police officers and the typical personality of an educator. Police officers are trained to maintain control over others. They protect themselves and the citizenry from people who want to do harm. By necessity, they are trained to use physical intimidation and restraint to maintain control. Typically, they are more aggressive and assertive than the average teacher.

Teachers, on the other hand, are looking to nurture rather than control. They want to find a good way forward for their students and are looking to provide opportunity for growth and learning in others. Opposite from a typical officer, they rely on persuasion and cooperation rather than aggression and restraint. I can relate well to this because, as a basketball coach and an athlete, I probably have more tendencies of a police officer than those of a teacher, especially when I was younger. In my early years of teaching, I often clashed in approach with my Education peers and, since confrontation wasn't out of my wheelhouse, I would often get my way. Fortunately, as I matured, I learned that there was great wisdom in the softer, gentler approach.

I have spent a lot of time trying to discover the path from "don't get that they don't get it" to "Oh, I get it." For example, I recently had a conversation with Bill, an inmate who works for the prison academy. He is a man in his 30s who had a fairly traditional youth, got lost in college, went down a perilous road and ended up in prison. Anyway, now he gets it. But, like all of us, there was a time when, "he didn't get that he didn't get it."

It all came clear to him as he was standing in the inmate yard in the prison in Draper watching the traffic pass on I-15. He had driven I-15 many times, looking disparagingly over at the lot that lived in prison. Now his perspective was completely opposite. For many years he didn't get it and he didn't get that he didn't get it. Suddenly he could finally see. I asked him what had changed. His response was interesting. He said, "It was surreal. I suddenly realized what I had done to myself, and my family."

"How could I have done this to them? What in me needed to change so that I would never do it again?"

"Every act I had done in my life over the past four years had hurt myself and them. It was painful."

"I committed then and there to not be that person anymore. I committed to become what my folks knew I could become."

"Mostly though, I committed to never do that to myself again. It is still painful, nearly every day, but with the pain comes a sense of redemption and purpose."

He continued, "The change was difficult. I felt like I was fighting the system the whole time. Sometimes it was easier to give in and I lost track of my real desire."

"UPrep and Education really make it easier to work at becoming my best self."

I think Bill sums up the process of realizing that you don't get that you don't get it. The same story appears in the story of the Prodigal Son in the New Testament. After spending his life and inheritance in riotous living, and finding himself at the very bottom of the barrel, his experience was summed up in a short verse. It simply says that the prodigal son, "…came to himself." Or, he came to the realization that he "didn't get that he didn't get it" and that he was responsible for his situation.

He thought for so long that he had all the answers. He was so sure that he knew what was best, that his parents or others were crazy. However, at that moment, truth came to his mind and he could see past the blinders and lies and realized where he needed to be and was willing to go there. The pride was gone and the journey home could begin. That realization comes every time a person changes, incarcerated or not.

Big changes require big realizations.

Brian Wood, formerly of Layton, was an inmate at the Central Utah Correctional Facility in Gunnison. He pleaded guilty to nine felony charges for offenses from 2011 to 2014, including counts of burglary, drug possession and prescription fraud.

In an article he wrote for the *Ogden Standard-Examiner*, Wood brought to light another aspect of this concept – personal accountability or owning your mistakes and choosing to move forward.

I have a friend here in prison, who said, "I'm probably the worst individual you've met in this place, because I actually did all the things I was accused of."
The humor in that is the fact so many prisoners minimize their crimes, make excuses, and play the victim.
I can't tell you how many times I've heard a prisoner tell the story of his crime, all the while highlighting how he was cheated by the system and treated unjustly only to then brag

about another crime he has committed and gotten away with. The irony blows my mind.

After hearing so many prisoners make excuses for their crimes, I have come to really detest this decidedly negative attribute, one I have been especially guilty of in the past. I had rationalized my bad behavior in many ways. The biggest excuse I came up with to explain my demise was that I went completely downhill after my wife left me because my world had been destroyed. All my legal trouble started then, and so, to many of my friends and acquaintances, this appeared to be the case.

Not only would I go along with this assumed explanation, I would outright lie about the situation. I claimed my wife left me completely out of the blue, and I simply fell apart after that. I would really play up my status as a victim in an effort to get sympathy from anyone who would listen.

The truth is my ex-wife left me because I was a drug addict and had been for years. Prescription pain killers became my main focus in life, and I let my marriage, career, family, friends and everything else in my life fall by the wayside.

The more I have heard so many excuses from other prisoners, the more I have tried to change this behavior in myself. And now, the more I have started to take full responsibility for my circumstances, the better I feel. When you keep telling lies you start to believe them. I had convinced myself I had somehow gotten a raw deal, and that notion had me miserable.

Feeling like a victim sucks. When I finally figured out all the bad things that have happened to me were because I had been a horrible human being, I felt quite liberated, because I knew I could change. After coming to that conclusion and facing my failures, I started focusing on solutions.

With as many prisoners that claim to be innocent, I am sure I have run across some that are. And while that's an upsetting thought, even they have the opportunity to decide how they will respond to their circumstances.

71

In that article, it is easy to see when Brian moved from a place of "people that don't get it don't get that they don't get it," to a realization of getting it. He left his artificial world of victimhood and entitlement and entered a world of accountability and transparency. Though it makes a person much more vulnerable, these perspectives are necessary steps to help that person "come to himself."

These attributes and characteristics apply to all of us. Somehow, before a person can progress, he or she *must* gain a sense of reality, accountability and realize the fact that they don't have all the answers. I was once told that the best way to find out what a person really knows is not in the answers he gives but in the questions he asks. I think that is true for all of us.

Bringing this idea to Corrections officers, it is interesting how many of them view themselves as educators. Some of them actually have more of that personality and could become quality educators. While in my experience, most of them don't fit the bill, nonetheless, they see themselves as understanding education and consider their educational efforts as effective. To understand the problem, imagine for a moment one of your favorite teachers. She is likely a kind, patient, directed, caring lady. Though I have many, I picture a former peer, Mrs. Liddell, (picture the actress Angela Lansbury). She was a dear lady with whom I taught for many years who had great talents as a teacher. Imagine her trying to don a blue uniform, holster a gun, mace, a Taser and handcuffs and go out in the community and enforce the law.

It wouldn't work.

Like many of my education peers, aside the now 34 years of experience, I attended four years of college, learning mathematics, computer science, physical science, and teaching techniques just to earn the privilege of teaching. Beyond that, I earned a Master's degree in Gifted and

Talented Education. Then I took another 45 credit hours working towards my administrative certificate (ASC). I don't claim that all that education was completely valuable. That's a topic for a different day. But I will say that it went a long way in helping me realize the nuances of becoming a quality educator and administrator. It wasn't easy. It was worth it.

Teaching is as much an art as it is a science. As with all skills, there are certain people who get it naturally. I have worked with many natural-born teachers. To them the process comes easy. They relate easily to their students. They realize there are many different learning styles. They naturally know that by creating personal interest in their students, their students will learn. When you take a natural-born teacher and give them some of the teaching techniques that make learning easier and you have a Mrs. Liddell-type teacher. I'm sure you can identify your own group of teachers who impacted your life. A good teacher can teach about any subject because they understand the art of teaching and will spend the time learning the details of what they are trying to teaching.

Although some of the officers assigned to Corrections' educational wing, Programming, whether as administrators or as officers, have some natural ability to teach, few really get it and none have the training or background. Those who get it do pretty well, but most don't and, well, it doesn't work. Because of that, the Programming world is full of junior league coaches that do their best and think they get it but really have little idea.

Even worse, many of those in administrative positions within Corrections are in the same boat. I really don't mean to be demeaning. We all find ourselves in the, "don't get that we don't get it" place in life from time-to-time. Getting out of that place into a place of self-realization is always a challenge. I believe any person to be successful in life must move into that realization over and over again. I think this will always be a problem for Corrections until they see the "elephant" for what it is. They must realize the importance of bringing in more qualified professionals to provide Programming as they have with Education or perhaps simply make educators responsible for Programming and allowing quality educators to direct the process. They must see beyond the "tail" to see the entire animal.

I might add that most of the officers in Programming are good people doing the best they can within an impossible system. In the current situation, concerning the processes in Programming, I don't understand why the academy, the Educational program of the Gunnison prison, is not responsible for the Programming classes taught by Corrections. That simple change would allow a more concerted, effective direction into the courses.

The biggest part of what they "don't get" is the entire second half of their mission statement:

Our team is devoted to providing maximum opportunities for offenders to make lasting changes through accountability, treatment, education, and positive reinforcement within a safe environment.

They talk the talk but they do not walk the walk. Not by a long shot. When asked about the HOPE program or Conquest or Programming, the UDOC administration tout their efforts and strengths. It reminds me of those Corrections/Education meetings I suffered through in the beginning of my tenure at the prison. Most people accept their perspective just like I did.

After several conversations with the Executive Director, I am convinced that he wants to do good things. He talks of reform and improvement. I believe he is even making real efforts to do such. However, it is clear that he doesn't want to move too fast, upset too many officers, or especially get in the way of the Inmate Placement Program (IPP). Sometimes gradual adjustments are appropriate. When a system is effective and working, making a huge change, tipping over the apple cart, is foolish. However, when the apple cart is full of rotten apples, the strategy is absolutely appropriate.

In my first coaching job, I inherited a program that was mediocre. I had been the assistant to the previous coach who was a fine man but had never spent much time in the coaching arena, though he carried the moniker. He really didn't delve into it or live it 100%, which I found is necessary to be successful in that field. That had been the tradition at that school for some time.

My first year at the reins, though a lot of what the previous coach had done was valid, I tipped over the apple cart. We started over, so to speak. I wanted the players to know that I was not going to accept the status quo. I wanted to win and I wanted to win immediately. For the most part the strategy worked. Although there were some prevailing attitudes and roadblocks we didn't overcome, we were successful and continued to be more and more so over the next nine years.

In my second coaching job, I inherited a program that had been successful for many years. It was one of the top schools in the classification. Though I wanted to change some things, I chose the gradual approach. I worked with some of the senior players and adopted some of the strategies they were familiar with and liked. It made more sense to keep a good ship running smoothly. We would implement our complete system over time.

Corrections is only succeeding 30% of the time. I think tipping over the apple cart is in order.

Chapter 13

ASCENT

Thee lift me, and I lift thee and we shall ascend together.
Linda K Burton

In the summer of 2016, about five years into my sentence, I received an invitation to a symposium to be held in an auditorium at Salt Lake Community College. It was an event sponsored by the UDOC under the direction of the governor to kick off a new program called ASCENT. Having spent the previous five years working with UDOC and going to the Corrections/Education quarterly meetings, I was not too enthusiastic. However, this seemed different. As a good soldier, I agreed to attend.

As I arrived at the auditorium in South Salt Lake, I was surprised at the number of people I recognized. Many were from the Gunnison prison. Others were from South Park. Others I had met at the Corrections/Education quarterly meetings. The auditorium was nearly full as we listened to speakers from all parts of the system.

There were multiple presenters from Corrections, from the state legislature and various other state agencies. The most interesting and engaging speaker, however, was a man who told the story of the violin (repeated from the first page of this book).

He was a felon with a difficult and tumultuous past. Though I do not remember his name, his story is well worth retelling.

His first memories are when he was about age three. He lived with his mother and younger sister in a rather remote place in Montana. Remote places are easy to find in that state. His mom had a live-in boyfriend who "took care of them." By age eight, he had a new baby brother and no longer had a boyfriend "dad." The man left for greener pastures. Unable to fend for herself, his mother moved with her kids to Ogden, Utah. They lived somewhere between Harrison Avenue and Washington Avenue. His mother worked and did the best she could but they were dirt poor. He went on to describe how different it was to go from a life of seclusion in Montana to the heart of what in Utah would be considered the inner city.

In a short time, he realized that there was a lot of opportunity available to him; most of it was of an unsavory nature. He started by finding a wardrobe off the clothes lines in the many backyards throughout the neighborhood. Looking for a faster way to get around, he found a bicycle to ride. Soon he realized that those bikes had a monetary value and that there were multiple buyers willing to pay him for his entrepreneurial efforts.

Before long he made his first trip to juvenile court. Those visits reoccurred many times for the next few years. By 14 he was in and out of juvenile detention. At 17 he did his first jail time. The trend continued and he received his first prison sentence for distribution of a controlled substance just before he turned 20.

He was now 29 and had been in and out of prison three times. He was once again standing before the judge about to return to prison for the fourth time. He was angry and more importantly, the judge was disgusted. Just before passing sentence, the judge asked him if he had anything to say.

His response started like this, "Yeah, can I ask you a question?"

"What?" replied the judge.

"Can I ask you a question?"

"What is it?" the judge responded impatiently.

Looking down at his feet and then back up at the judge, he asked, "Can you play the violin?"

77

"No," came the response.

"What if I told you that you have to play *The Star Spangled Banner* on the violin. Could you do it?"

Again the response came back with an emphatic, "No!"

"What if I put a gun to your head and threatened to pull the trigger if you failed to play *The Star Spangled Banner*. Could you do it?"

"No! What's the point?" decried the judge.

"And if I threatened your family, could you play it then?"

Completely impatient, the judge nearly shouted, "No! I can't play the violin under any circumstances. I never learned how. What is the point?"

Again, looking at the ground in front of him, the convicted drug dealer responded, "I don't know how to live a good life. Can you teach me?"

From that exchange, the judge determined that there was a definite lack in this man's understanding of how to live an honest, honorable life. Rather than sentence him to prison for the fourth time, he placed him in a rehab program with certain requirements and limitations.

To finish the story, that exchange with the judge was eight years prior to the ASCENT symposium where he was speaking. The man now has a family: a beautiful wife with two children. He owns a business and is a positive contributor to society and has been for more than six years. The man had come to a point of getting that he didn't get it. He "...came to himself" and was ready for change.

At the end of the symposium, I was asked to participate on the newly formed Education and Employment committee. We held our first meeting and were given the basic outline of ASCENT and the purpose of our committee. These are the notes from that first meeting in the summer of 2016:

Current Statistics:

- Nationally in 2005, 698,000 inmates were released from prison.
- 67% were rearrested and returned to prison.
- Total state expenditures for prison and transition programs in 2011 was $52 billion.
- One-third of adult offenders have a diagnosable mental illness.
- 75% of adult offenders have a substance abuse problem.
- 40% of released offenders do not have a GED or high school diploma.
- Only one-third of the inmates receive any vocational training while incarcerated.
- 55% of inmates have children under age 18.

A new program, Transition Accountability Plan Goals and Process (TAP), starts during an offender's classification and admission to prison and continues until discharge in the community.

- TAP defines the programs or interventions needed to modify risk factors of the offender.
- Appropriate partners should participate in the development and implementation of TAP.
- TAP becomes a long-term road map for services.

This was the vision of the state's new program, ASCENT. Over the long haul, these partnerships will build broader political support for transition reform by engaging state and local officials, agency leaders, community leaders, crime victims, faith-based and non-profit organizations and offenders and their families.

ASCENT Goal

The overarching goals of ASCENT are for all criminal justice involved clients/offenders, county, state or federal, from intake through release, to remain arrest free over the long haul and to become competent and self-sufficient members of their community.

ASCENT Objectives

To promote public safety by reducing the threat of harm to persons and their property by offenders who have been released in the communities to which they return by improving opportunities for real change throughout the incarceration process.

Challenges for Transition
- Lack of focus on offender success as a desired outcome.
- Lack of consensus that transition should begin at admission to prison and extend through discharge.
- Extreme fragmentation within agencies managing transition.
- Lack of offender programs/interventions.

I left that meeting thinking that perhaps there was hope for the struggling Corrections system. The entire 2-hour drive home was occupied with hope and ideas and potential. Though I had read the UDOC mission statement many times, this was the first time I had seen in them a desire to move towards that statement's goals in a large scale. I had seen and heard individual officers, wardens, etc. express their desire to move in that direction and in fact had seen them take steps to that effect. Although there were times they would encourage and support efforts we were making at the Gunnison prison academy, I had long given up hope that any large-scale change was possible.

This seemed different.

For the next six months, I sat on the Education and Employment committee. There were representatives from the Utah Department of Correction, Utah DOWD, the Utah State Office of Education, the Department of Workforce Services, and multiple community business owners with a desire to throw in ideas and create change. Between monthly ASCENT meetings, I collaborated with our inmate council. They were a treasure trove of great ideas.

Over that time, our inmate council developed what we affectionately referred to as the Comprehensive Recidivism Reduction, Education, and Employment Plan (CRREEP). That acronym was created by the inmate council. Perhaps it is inappropriate but they really liked it and wanted it included that way.

Our monthly meetings were very exciting. I felt we were given the charge to present real options for change and improvement. The modification of the outline we created in that committee is included in this book.

However, in January of the following year, changes were made in the leadership of the committee. The previous UDOC representative who served as committee chairman was retiring and was being replaced by the captain of UCI. The January meeting took on a completely different tone. My objections and those of the business owners and educators went unnoticed. Rather than pursue the idea of real reform that had a hope of providing the needed path to solving the problems, things went back to the old, Education/Corrections meetings lovefests I had had to suffer through for years. From the new UDOC chairman's perspective, we were doing all we could do so we should celebrate our successes. (Sounds familiar doesn't it?)

At the meeting in March, I voiced my objection. About half of the committee worked for the UDOC in some fashion or another and would not join me. Myself and the other educators and the business people were on board, however. We re-presented our outline of CRREEP as well as an outline of a tiered progression proposal we had put together during our committee time prior to "Captain Train Wreck." At the conclusion of our presentation, that captain looked at me and said, "We need to focus our efforts on what we can control and maintain right now."

Unfortunately, that was the last meeting I attended. Though the committee still meets, it has had no impact of any kind that I can see.

I determined that I would no longer waste my time with leadership that had all the right answers to all the wrong questions. This leadership "doesn't get that he doesn't get it." For better or for worse, I decided to take the advice; I came back to CUA and focused on the things I could control; CUA and UPrep.

The outline of the products of the ASCENT committee before it was train wrecked can be found in Chapter 29, titled "A Real Solution" of this book. I believe it is the outline of a program that would have helped the young man who asked about the violin. I am confident it would create a major culture change as well as a major process change within the UDOC that would allow many, many more offenders to learn how to live a good life. As of June 2019, it would take very little to apply it to CUCF either in the way of money or manpower. Control of the process would have to be given to someone who truly has a vision of the desired outcomes. The Corrections staff would have to change their paradigm, (something I believe most would gladly do). The UDOC powers that be would also have to change their perspective in a drastic way. Unfortunately, I don't see that happening.

This is the Justification part of the ASCENT document we created.

JUSTIFICATION

Our system completely fails society and inmates by releasing them without support and education. Though best efforts are made everywhere in the current situation, there is no real process or REQUIRED process in place.

It took most of these men YEARS to get where they are. It is reasonable to expect it would take years to change them. The violin analogy given at the ASCENT symposium is a perfect example of what is required to provide opportunity for change.

Just like the violin analogy, an individual must **want to learn** to play. They must **receive proper training**. They must **practice, fail and try again**. They must **receive more support and instruction**.

They must **play in front of others** and learn to deal with that pressure. They must have a **continual desire to improve**. They must **feel good about their process**. They must be, over extended time, taught and **prepared to perform in public**. Parole should be the climax of a process of change, similar to a violin recital. *Expecting a parolee to perform as a citizen without the necessary preparation is exactly like asking someone to play a violin concert without preparation.* Failure will be imminent.

People want to be better. People want to perform. People want to be productive. Many people just don't know how. Let the inmates buy into the process. Let them realize they have a chance. Provide them **real hope** and **real purpose** and they will **choose** to change.

If implemented, this process will be less expensive and more productive. Our recidivism rates will drop.

This will not apply to all inmates. Some will not want to change. If an inmate refuses to take the steps before him, he chooses to serve out his complete sentence. As they choose to change and take advantage of the opportunities before them, we will have moved much closer to finding lasting solutions for individuals as well as society. I believe we owe this to society, the inmates, and even their victims. Many victims don't want their perpetrator to ever get out. I'm not sure I blame them. However, if they are going to parole and get out early, some solace would be provided in that they had actually taken real steps to reform.

Chapter 14

Sex and Drugs and Rock-n-Roll

*You start out playing rock-n-roll so you can have sex
and do drugs, but you end up doing drugs so you can still
play rock-n-roll and have sex.*

Mick Jagger

In 1981, I was living in Perpignan, France. It was an amazing city just off the Mediterranean Coast about 30 kilometers from Spain. I was doing missionary service for the church I belong to and was working in the Perpignan area. My companion, Gary, was from England. I spent over six months in that beautiful city and over four months with him, who proved to be one of my favorite companions during my two-year stay in southern France.

He was British, which was a new experience for me. Up to that point, all of my companions had been Americans with mostly similar backgrounds as myself: conservative, western United States, etc. Gary was from a different culture, which was an exciting change for me. He was a "what you see is what you get" kind of person, very authentic and also very free spirited. During those 4 months we worked very hard but we also had a lot of fun. He enjoyed life and helped me learn to do the same, sometimes too much so.

Along with our day-to-day missionary responsibilities, we were responsible to provide support to about 50 other missionaries spread out along the Mediterranean coast from Perpignan to Montpellier to Carcassonne, a medieval city about 60 kilometers inland. (I know, it sounds like a vacation, right?) Part of that support meant visiting them and working with them.

In June of that year, we determined to visit missionaries in Montpellier, a trip of about 160 kilometers. We jumped on the train and arrived at the Montpellier train station. The missionaries who were supposed to meet us were nowhere to be found. We were new to the city so we only had an address and a map. Being both of the adventurous type, rather than grab a taxi, we looked at the map and decided we could make it on foot.

As we worked our way through the center of town, we noticed a billboard advertising a visit from an English punk rock band. Though I cannot remember their name, I remember thinking, "Who on earth would like this crap? Weird haircuts, colored hair – not for me." My version of good music came from the Rock Genre; Kiss, Queen, Eric Clapton, anything out of 70s Rock.

Well, come to find out, Gary did like punk rock! He started to go nuts. He got wild-eyed and started walking, nearly jogging, toward the small stadium where the event was to occur. Before long we could see some oddly dressed guys with spiked green, red and blue hair moving towards the stage. Now we were running.

As fate would have it, this was a punk rock band Gary was very familiar with. He was a Punk Rocker of sorts, which was a revelation to me. It was all very entertaining. It took great effort to bring him back to earth and to the purpose of our visit to Montpellier. Finally, we set out to meet our missionary friends.

From that time forward it was not uncommon for Gary to break out singing the song, "Sex and Drugs and Rock-n-Roll" by Ian Dury and the Blockheads. It became such a common occurrence that though I have never heard that song played by the original band, or any band for that matter, I can, to this day, recite a good portion of the lyrics, thanks to listening to Gary's intermittent breakouts into song. "Sex and drugs and rock n roll is all my brain and body need. Sex and drugs and rock n roll is very good indeed." There's more but I'll spare you the details.

Interestingly, his singing didn't put me off. Though we were missionaries trying to teach the idea that moderation and self-control were critical to happiness, rather than rampant sex and drug use, I found it entertaining and harmless. However, experience has taught me that such an attitude of "Sex and Drugs and Rock-n-Roll" is not harmless. There are extensive, long-term, and societal as well as personal consequences.

I tell that story because it leads into the world of prisons. I have had conversation with hundreds of inmates. Though I never ask what they did that got them to prison, often I asked what got them started down a bad road. Without exception, every one of them found the beginning of their plight in drugs, alcohol, or pornography, or all three.

It is not the purpose of this writing to be a moral authority or suggest we find a way to eliminate drugs, alcohol or pornography from our society. Though I believe, and in fact am sure, that without those three vices, prisons would be nearly empty. I realize this to be a topic for another day. However, I also believe that identifying these three substances as the beginning of the demise of all these people, and many others not incarcerated, is worth a discussion.

Looking the other way will not help resolve the problems plaguing our society. It is interesting to me that many people are quick to blame guns for the violence across America. They claim that eliminating or controlling guns would resolve so many societal problems. I argue that gun violence is not near the problem nor does it result in near the hurt and victimization, as do drugs, alcohol and pornography. In fact, I believe that gun violence, like all other crimes, often has at its core one or more of these three substances.

Taking from my conversations with many of the incarcerated men I have worked with, a good portion of them would give anything to be able to go back and never start down that road of sex and drugs and rock n roll. My grandpa once told me that, "The one way to guarantee you will never become an alcoholic is to never drink alcohol."

The inmate Bill, whom I referenced earlier told me that, "If my experience helps my cousins or my brother or anyone in my family avoid this ugly road I followed, it was well worth it; but it is still really, really painful."

From my conversations with a variety of inmates, one or more of these three things in a sense took away their ability to choose. Not to imply that the individual is not responsible for his or her choices; on the contrary. Choice and accountability are critical to any person's success and likewise can directly result in any person's failure. Nonetheless, they chose to give away their ability to choose as their addictions controlled their desires and their actions. Choice is one of the fundamental gifts mankind has been given. Addictions take that away. Nothing but following the addiction matters. Again, I'm not meaning to imply that they are not responsible for their actions. Just the opposite. But when that choice is effectively taken away because of addiction, outcomes change from potentially good to almost always bad. Heartache and failure follow.

In spite of their repeated failures, there exists a group of inmates who can't wait to get back to regular drug use. A lot of these men have access to some drugs in prison, (go figure) but miss the daily high they can get when they are on the streets. The problem is, being able to afford these near constant highs requires them to have money and since their drug activity often makes it impossible to hold down any kind of a quality job, they have to resort to illegal activity to get the money they need for their fix. Even when they clear their head, for various reasons, they can't leave the lifestyle.

Here I would like to share a column from a former felon who writes articles for the *Ogden Standard-Examiner*, Brian

Wood. He served four years in the Utah State prison system before being released on parole on Jan. 2, 2018.
It is a telling story about addiction and how some people can change and perhaps why some don't.

What do prisoners dream about doing when they are released? Last week, I wrote about my vacation and scratching some things off my freedom list. These things are often a topic of discussion in prison. You'd expect prisoners to romanticize about food and women, and they do, but neither come close to the most vocally fantasized aspect of freedom: drugs. It would always amaze me at just how many prisoners' Number One expressed desire was to get high.

I can't really provide a catchall explanation of why some choose to quit and others never will. In my experience thus far, you know before the inmate gets out whether they are going back to drugs or not. I'm yet to be surprised by a parolee either way. That's good news for the guys who have really decided not to use anymore. Unfortunately, the number of guys who make that choice is pretty low, and the reasons why others don't quit run the spectrum.

One life-long meth user gave me a simple explanation as to why he never plans to quit: "I love it." He had a positive outlook on his situation, but his judgment was probably a bit off. I suspect that was due to the meth. He explained each time he went to prison, it gave his body a much needed rest and healing period. He boasted that prison helped him stay looking good and young — of which, he looked neither. I also suspect that was due to the meth. He went on to explain that nothing in the world is better than that first time you get high after not having it for years, another benefit to incarceration.

I could somewhat understand the position of a guy who felt the positives of getting high outweighed the negatives. I respected that more than the guys who claimed they would "try" to stay off drugs. Those guys often found themselves high the first day as well, but the difference was the guy who hadn't lied to himself had waited until after he met with the parole officer. I've seen plenty of both.

Then there's the group I feel bad for and there's plenty of them in prison. They might express good intentions at some time, but they really aren't capable. Most of these guys have some sort of mental illness issue or other cognitive disadvantage. Many have never known any other life. Disabilities are a reality and just like someone's inability to walk, some have an inability to reason, [thus] affecting their judgment and decision making. We are not created equal.

There are a number of prisoners who are just more comfortable in prison and prefer it there. I watched a guy who received an unexpected time cut fall into an immediate depressed state. He told me he didn't want to drink, but knew he would end up doing it. He figured, "Might as well be the first day, why fight it?" He had given up on the idea of being a functional member of society a long time ago. He didn't even want to tell his family he was getting out. He figured he could be back in before they even knew it.

A lot of prisoners have anxiety when they are getting close to leaving. Many feel the hopes of success their friends and families have for them are a burden. They don't want to let everyone down again and they stress out knowing they will. Unfortunately, it seems the desire to get high often outweighs their desire to succeed.

People do drugs because it feels amazing! At least it does in the beginning. Eventually the "high" turns into getting back to feeling normal, or just not being sick. But definitely at first, I did drugs because it felt wonderful. I don't believe people stay addicted to a drug after being away from drugs for years. I think what they have is a perfect knowledge of how it will feel to do the drug, and, in a lot of instances, that is enough to make people dismiss the consequences, even with a perfect knowledge of the consequences.

So why do some prisoners dream of healthy activities and some dream of drugs? I know I can never reach a physical euphoria equal to what could be achieved with chemicals, and I'm content knowing that. I believe the consequences I garnered were enough. Each situation is unique. Some just love drugs too much, some don't have a hope of a better life, and others just haven't experienced enough consequences... yet.

The problem lies back in the idea that "people that don't get it don't get that they don't get it." Whether it is the person who becomes addicted and loses his choice or the person who uses any of these substances though not addicted, commits terrible acts, the lack of realization of the problem and the unwillingness to admit it is both a personal problem for that individual and a societal problem for the rest of us.

I don't know the answer to drug abuse, alcohol abuse or pornography addiction. I don't think that everyone that drinks, views porn or smokes dope is necessarily a bad person or will eventually end up in prison. That is definitely not the case. I only know that these substances are the plagues of the modern age. The prison population is proof enough of that.

Chapter 15

The Culture Problem

It's really a wonder that I haven't dropped all my ideals,
because they seem so absurd and impossible to carry out.
Yet I keep them, because in spite of everything,
I still believe that people are really good at heart.

Anne Frank

One of the most difficult obstacles we had to take head-on was the culture of the officers within the Department of Corrections. I have met and had conversations with a large portion of the officers at CUCF. They are good people who find themselves in a difficult position. I cannot imagine the challenge of going to work every day with little purpose and even less hope. Picture yourself going, every day, to a job that amounts to little more than babysitting adults. Though there are certain officer jobs that allow for more than that, for the most part, you would sit in a bubble and open and close doors, take requests from inmates for everything from mail problems, to commissary orders, to complaints/grievances. There would be little in the way of achievement or accomplishment. You would literally act as a babysitter, except the "babies" aren't all that cute.

As stated earlier, the recidivism rate among felons in Utah is in the neighborhood of 70%, a very poor number. The retention rate for officers in the UDOC is nearly as bad. It is estimated that fewer than 40% of officers last more than 3 years. There is a constant effort to find new recruits. For rural Utah, the pay is pretty good. I know the people at CUCF and they are good people. However, the work environment is terrible.

To date, the Draper Prison is short 157 officers. The prison at Gunnison doesn't suffer the same staffing issues but the Draper shortage is "shared" by the officers in Gunnison. In addition, Corrections is looking to turn many responsibilities done by officers over to civilian staff to save money. Makes no sense (unless it was Corrections turned over to educators).

I was fortunate to enjoy 34 years in public education. Though there were challenges and times I wondered if I really wanted to coach and teach, except for a two and a half year period, I enjoyed my job. I looked forward to Mondays and I felt I had a positive effect on the world I lived in. My work life, though on a set schedule, was always different, filled with challenges and opportunities all around. I don't know that all my colleagues had the same experience and I know that teacher retention in public education in Utah is only in the 75% range. But that is a result of too much headache for the pay, instead of too much boredom. I believe that boredom is at the heart of the UDOC culture problem. I'd like to give several examples.

It is not uncommon to hear officers brag about making inmates wait at a slider to leave their section, just for the fun of it.

To better explain, there are two kind of doors in CUCF. Cell doors have no "call button" and are opened and closed by requirement. Inmates cannot "request" those doors to be opened or closed. Some inmates, with high permission levels, have their cell doors opened early in the morning and except for lockdowns, those doors remain open all day, well into the evening. They can go in and out of their cell into their section, (a small shared area just outside their cell with tables and a TV). Lockdowns come for a variety of reasons, mostly from inmates fighting. They can also happen for other security reasons like power outages, etc.

Inmates with lower permission levels must be in their cells earlier in the day. The doors are closed until the following morning.

Most of the other doors in the facility have a "call button" that when pushed, alerts the officer that someone wants to go through the door. Those doors are at all intersections; to leave their section, to leave the bubble area, to leave the unit corridor, to go into visiting, to go into programing hallways, etc. The inmate arrives at the door, pushes the call button at his own risk and waits for the door to open.

It was not uncommon for me to be in a housing unit working with caseworkers or captains or even inmates and, on my way to leave, arrive at the popper or slider – the door to leave the unit – where several inmates waited, sometimes for several minutes, for the door to open. I would arrive, push the button, and the door would open rather quickly. Later, as we all walked down the corridor together, they would make a comment about me "having the magic touch" to get the doors open.

Clearly it was not uncommon for them to wait on a regular basis. This didn't happen all the time. However, the fact that it happened at all was bothersome. Though it could be that the officer was "busy" and couldn't get to the switch to open the door, it is unlikely as the large majority of the time officers are "bored" and have little to do but monitor corridors from a video screen.

Teasing or perhaps bullying of this type occurs more than it should. It is referred to by inmates as "poking the bear." They have to be very careful with some officers. Say the wrong thing to the wrong officer and the consequences could be dire. A classic example of that happened to Reggie. I mentioned him earlier; the man who shot the predator stalking his daughter. Reggie was living in Cedar housing unit in a privileged section. He had been in prison about two years or so and knew the rules. An officer had a power surge and started "poking a stick" at him. Reggie finally had enough and took it up with the Cedar Lieutenant. Shortly afterwards, this officer and company "tossed" Reggie's cell looking for anything they could find. It was a clear attempt to provoke him. Before it was over, he found himself spending a week in SMU, (Special Management Unit). The officer was gonna "show" him and did. Again, with some officers, that is a regular occurrence. I believe that kind of authoritarian behavior is a result of culture. This type of officer behavior, though not outwardly encouraged, is not discouraged, either.

Another example that happened in the summer of 2019 occurred in a housing unit. Two officers were accosted by two inmates. One officer was restrained by a first inmate while the second inmate pummeled the second officer. Upon conversation with several caseworkers, I was told that the inmate, who is a member of a gang, didn't want to take a UA (Urine Analysis) to test for drugs, so he beat up the officer. As a consequence, the inmate that pummeled the officer will be "thrown in the hole" for eight years. That means he will be in as restricted environment as allowed by law for eight years. That is the official version.

The real version is that the officer who was pummeled had been poking the bear for some time. The gang shot-caller (leader) had enough and ordered the hit. There are several clear indicators that this is the more accurate version. First, being that, inside a prison, a gang member does nothing out of line without being told to by his shot caller. They are given strict orders. I have seen multiple versions of the written decrees from gang leaders to obey the prison rules, go to school, etc. They don't always comply but they never cross a line and beat somebody, inmate or officer, without direction from the shot caller. Second, the inmate knew full well that beating up a guard would result in eight years in the hole. To think that he would give up eight years because he didn't want to take a UA is ridiculous. The consequences of failing a UA are extremely minor compared to that of beating a guard.

This example illustrates two flaws in the current system. The first is this officer's treatment of the inmates. Poke a bear long enough and he's gonna fight back. The second is that Corrections doesn't address the problem. Why aren't officers who continually "poke the bear" identified and corrected? It's not hard to spot. But to change a culture, you have to change thinking and behavior.

One of the most blatant occurrences of culture issues that I personally witnessed came at the graduation ceremony in 2018. Each summer, like most schools, the prison academy hosts a graduation. Typically, there are between 40 and 70 graduates. We host a traditional ceremony with student and guest speakers. One of those speakers comes from the UDOC. That year, one of the assistant wardens drew the short straw and was selected to speak. Nearly all of the speakers from other years who represented the UDOC had done a fine job, but this year was different. In a nutshell, he explained to the graduates, with many of their families in the audience, that they were worthless, had no value, no hope, and didn't deserve this or anything. I was dumbfounded. I was also embarrassed for the Utah Department of Corrections. Thankfully, I was the last speaker and could repair some of the damage.

It was crazy that one of the lead administrators of that facility could have such a narrow vision of what they were supposed to be doing. I wanted to take out the UDOC mission statement and ask him to read it. It is easy to see that if a deputy warden had that perspective, the officers under his supervision would have a similar one.

During the last several months of my tenure at the prison academy when it became known that my retirement was imminent, many of the officers who I had worked closely with over the years made comments about the culture problems. A large number of them thanked me for the work we had done. In that thanks they expressed the idea that when I "fished" in some eight years ago, they thought I was crazy using terms like maverick, nuts, didn't get it, and clueless. Many of them explained that before I showed up, they did not see value in their job, that they had no enjoyment. From their comments, it was clear that we had helped them gain a greater appreciation for what they were doing.

Some felt they were now accomplishing something and their jobs were more enjoyable. The idea of requiring education for all undereducated inmates was something they had never considered possible or even needed. The idea of including education compliance in order to be eligible to hold a job or receive a Prison Matrix Level (PML) advancement was something they thought impossible to enforce. They worried that having all those inmates, some 250 per hour in the Education corridor of 10 classrooms, would be a security nightmare. Mostly, they thought there would be a huge inmate "rebellion." According to the officers, "The inmates would never do it willingly." That statement really caught me off guard. We found, over the years that not only would the inmates cooperate, the large majority of them cooperated with us without much objection.

An example of that was in our standardized testing. When I first "fished" in, there were about 200 students total in CUA. Recruiting students was a nightmare. In the early days I would go from section to section inquiring about interest. Our efforts to gain new students and to get them to TABE test failed miserably.

Fast forward less than two years. We had developed a testing center in the Education corridor. Rather than taking the testing on the road, we brought our student inmates to the testing center to test. Up until the time I retired, it was not uncommon to see a dozen inmates patiently standing in line for the opportunity to take the TABE test. They were there willingly. There was no anger. There was no high emotion or animosity. There was only willingness to participate. In less than 18 months, we had completely changed the culture of education within the entire prison. Over time, the inmates came to realize that CUA was a place of hope and opportunity. Currently, over 80% of the prison population at CUCF is directly involved in CUA either as a student, employee or volunteer. Almost all the rest have completed all their high school requirements including functioning above a 12th grade level in reading, language and math. Though there are still a few that we couldn't get to, we have changed the culture of CUA. Sadly, the culture of CUCF has not completely followed suit. Though improvements have been made, there are still miles to go.

Eight years ago, trying to help inmates improve was considered heresy and except for a few locations like the STRIVE program, inmates were always marginalized. Now there is still STRIVE and also a new housing unit called Ironwood. Both currently have excellent captains who see value in a better approach and are working to effect change in their inmates. Other housing units have implemented programs that require productive time from inmates, 20 to 40 hours per week in which individuals are required to engage a minimum amount of time doing something productive. I believe it is making a positive difference in the entire facility. Sadly, all are not in agreement and even sadder, the UDOC structure remains in disarray with the tail wagging the dog. On the disheartened side, from conversations with my former staff, CUCF administration is pushing to undo much of the progress made.

This is another perspective of Inmate Edmond on the subject:

After a little more than two months in R&O I was transferred to CUCF in Gunnison, Utah. I was actually looking forward to the transfer. By now I had observed that most of the hard cases like gang members and violent offenders preferred the Draper prison to the one in Gunnison. The so-called "squares" and "new fish" all wanted to go to the "softer" prison. It had a lot more opportunities for Programming and Education. All Draper had to offer was "gladiator" school.

Within minutes of arriving in Gunnison I was relieved of my shackles and handcuffs. I noticed the place was immaculate and well groomed. It almost felt like entering into a country club in comparison to Draper. Within half an hour they had taken my picture, printed off an ID, given me a urinalysis, handed me a brief orientation packet and sent me to my housing unit without an escort. When I got to the housing unit, I was given a cell number and told to settle in by an officer who couldn't be seen behind the reflective film on the control room bubble. I walked into the section and all eyes were on me for a brief moment. Then as quickly as they focused on me, they went back to what they were doing. A couple guys were on the phone. A half dozen guys were huddled around the TV watching a movie. A couple guys were playing ping pong. The rest were either working out, playing cards or isolated in their cells watching their own TVs. It felt very much like a college dorm. There was no officer presence except for the occasional walk through. It was a welcome relief.

Upon getting settled in, several inmates approached me and gave me the 411 on the section and the prison as a whole. No one knew me so they immediately wanted to know what my charges were. Once they could see that I wasn't a sex offender, they proceeded to point out all the sex offenders. Clearly this environment was much different than Draper. That being said, there were some strong similarities. Sex offenders were allowed to coexist in some of the housing units but were all considered PARIAH. If you weren't one of them then you were expected to ignore them. You were supposed to treat them like they didn't exist. As a new fish I was given all kinds of advice; do this, don't do that. The rules for being a convict seemed endless and those were inmates' rules. I did my best to take it all in stride. Anything I didn't learn today I was certainly going to learn tomorrow. My safety counted on it. When I wasn't certain about something, I made sure to ask. This accomplished two things. First it made the others feel important and second it kept me out of trouble. I had learned from my R&O experience that to find out the pecking order was vital to survival.

First thing the following day I made the trip down to the Programming and Education corridors. I filled my schedule with classes. The only time I spent in my cell was during count at 11 am and 4 pm and from 6 pm to 5:30 am when breakfast was served. At that time I had an entry level Privilege Matrix Level (PML) of IL1. The first letter indicates the time you have to be in cell. The second letter dictates all your other privileges like commissary, phone calls and visits. The number at the end is the number of months you have before you can apply for a PML increase. It requires about six months to earn all levels and be classified as a KQ5, the highest PML. KQ5's can be out of cell each day until 10 pm, spend up to $65 a week on commissary, have unlimited phone calls and have up to 16 contact visits each month.

After my first 30 days I put in for my first PML increase. Ironically it was denied because the caseworker was unaware of the classes I was attending. At the time, one of their requirements to advance levels was to be attending at least one Education or Programming class. I was in 2 of both but their system couldn't keep track of it. It took nearly a week to get everything straightened out. In the end the caseworkers excuse was that Programming and Education had not updated the information on the computer. I asked her why she didn't call me into her office and ask about my involvement. She responded that she goes by the computer, right or wrong and that she wouldn't believe an inmate anyway. She declared that she wasn't a babysitter. Her message came through loud and clear.

Is there hope for change? I hope so. I believe the current Executive Director to be a good person who will look for ways to improve. However, from our conversation, both in person and email, it is clear that this office is clouded with politics and inaccurate assessments. For example, in our most recent face-to-face conversation, I mentioned a program located in downtown Salt Lake City called The Other Side Academy. It is an amazing program that is NOT government funded. It is a privately funded program that takes individuals who are headed to prison, are in drug rehab programs, or are living on the streets and engages them in a multi-year, residential program teaching them soft skills, job skills, and principles of self-reliance. Last I checked, they have a near perfect record for rehabilitation. I could go into detail here but a visit to their website, https://www.theothersideacademy.com will answer any questions you may have.

Anyway, back to the conversation with the Director. He had little good to say about the program. He stated that "they must have someone in the state legislature that backs them or they wouldn't exist." In his opinion, they are off the rails. In my opinion, they are exactly the type of program that the prison system should adopt for any inmate who wants to work towards parole. They are spot on!

Another example of the leadership missing the mark is the perception of the county jail, Inmate Placement Program (IPP). I go into more detail about that program later in this book. In short, it is a program in which many of the county jails around the state were able to build jail facilities to support their local needs by providing beds for state inmates. In statements to me and to the press, leadership stated that those jail programs provide the same programs and opportunities that are provided at CUCF. I have worked with most of the directors of those jails over the previous eight years. Most of them are good people trying to do the best that they can. However, except for a small handful, the directors of those jails are mostly hog-tied either with uncooperative jail staff or completely inadequate physical facilities. In addition to CUA, I was responsible for the Education program inside the Sanpete County Jail. A CUA staff member would go in two nights a week, for a total of about 6 hours. Though the jail commander and staff were great to work with and would accommodate any reasonable request, the opportunities were nothing near what is available at CUA. The teacher could only have 5 inmates at a time in her very small classroom. There were a limited number of books and computers as well. Similar problems exist throughout the state's county jail system. With a few exceptions, learning/Programming services in county are nothing compared to what is available at CUA.

Because of these and many more culture problems, any effort to turn the current prison system into a Corrections system will require a complete makeover, not with facilities as much as with focus and expected outcomes from the security staff and leadership. It's interesting that there is a desperate need to change the attitudes and behavior of inmates, preparing them to be employable citizens with the ability to live in a civil society. Before that can happen, the attitudes of the security staff and leadership also have to be changed.

As mentioned, this could be done with very few additional dollars in the short term and would save millions of dollars in the long run, to say nothing of changing thousands of lives.

Chapter 16

The Ordeal of Change

The victim mindset dilutes the human potential.
By not accepting personal responsibility
for our circumstances, we greatly reduce
our power to change them.

Steve Maraboli

As I sat in church one Sunday, I heard a man say that his mother had, for years, kept a quote on her fridge for all in the family to see: "Every Saint has a Past and Every Sinner has a Future."

As I thought on the idea and mixed it with my experiences at CUCF, I decided that nothing could be truer about the human condition.

It is not uncommon for any of us to find ourselves in a position of hopelessness. Perhaps it's from something we've done that we feel is catastrophic or perhaps something we didn't do. Maybe somebody has done something that has created devastation or challenge in our lives. Perhaps it is circumstance or bad luck. No matter the cause, we have all had times of worthlessness and feeling there is no way forward. Feelings of failure and defeat can be overpowering.

We have all made our mistakes. We have all had our failures. We have all been "sinners." Likewise, in our own rights, we have all done things well. We have all had our successes. We have all been "saints." Change is the key ingredient to life. We are always changing either for the better or the worse; we never stay the same. Not our personalities, not our bodies, nor our intellect. We are always in evolution. The same is true for inmates. The real key to what life has ahead of us isn't so much where we have been but is about the direction we are headed.

Most people's lives are full of choice and self-selection. That is the way we change and hopefully grow. We come to a crossroads, make a decision and learn from the consequences. Though that is a simplistic explanation, that is the pattern. Without choice, there is no growth. Without hope, the possibility of changing is very limited. This pattern is not a new development nor is it a ground-breaking discovery. It is life. That being said, the only way for a person to move forward, felon or not, is to have hope, purpose, choice and self-selection.

If the Utah Department of Corrections wants to do any correcting, they are going to have to integrate hope, purpose, choice, and self-selection into their system. Currently there exists almost none of any of these.

I realize that these men have done something terrible to be incarcerated. I realize that they may not "deserve" anything. I realize that some people they have hurt may never fully recover. No matter the cause or excuse, the damage is done. That cannot be changed. What *can* be potentially changed is the future behavior of these men. Over 95% of them will be released from prison either on parole or from expiration. If we do nothing, they will just hurt someone else and end up back in prison. That is the current pattern and it is … foolish.

The UDOC sits in the perfect position to effect the kind of change needed. The problem is they are not really the UDOC (Utah Department of Corrections). They are the UDOP (Utah Department of Prisons). Inmates taking a class on "Victim Impact" or a course on "Thinking for a Change" looks good on paper, but in and of itself has little effect. It is similar to taking a course in college. I have spent my share of life in school. My most recent experience was earning my administrative endorsement to be an administrator in a public school. I took about 45 credit hours of course work on everything ranging from Grant Writing to Constructive Leadership in Schools. I learned a lot about concepts. However, it wasn't until I could put some of what I learned into practice, to try and fail and try again that I developed the leadership skills I needed to be effective. In addition, I had many examples, some good and some bad, that shaped my learning path and my philosophy as a school administrator. All that to learn the task of administration. I would dare say that changing/learning proper basic behavior when a person has gone so far wrong as to find himself in prison is a much more complicated and drawn-out process than earning a college degree.

Yet, the UDOC thinks it can be done "a year from the gate" by taking a few classes and making a few commitments.

Change takes time. Personal improvement takes determined, consistent, long-term effort and commitment. It is not easy and there are no magic solutions. There are no shortcuts. The UDOC laments their troubles with the current transition programs, that their Adult Probation and Parole (AP&P) officers are overloaded and they need more resources for transition. What if they started their "transition" program the day a person was incarcerated? What if to be eligible for parole, an inmate had to put himself on a designed path to parole that lasted years and followed defined, measurable steps requiring accountability and personal growth? What if correcting behavior was at the heart of Corrections?

One of the conditions at the heart of the problem is that the majority of inmates consider themselves victims. Though that sounds strange, it is true. A victim is someone who either real or imagined, is at the mercy of another; someone whose life is controlled by someone else. All of us have the potential of being victims. We may be victims of a crime or victims of a car accident, or victims of verbal or physical abuse. We may be victims of circumstance or victim of an untold number of causes. We may be victims of our own foolishness. If we are not careful, we let these things control us and we fall into a victim mentality. Most inmates find themselves as victims.

If you have read *The Diary of Anne Frank* or any other history of the Holocaust, you will know that victimhood is a choice, one that each of us makes every day.

In the criminal world, the opposite of a victim is a perpetrator. To someone being verbally abused, the opposite of a victim is an abuser. I would more generally conclude that the opposite of a victim is a producer. In a perfect world, that producer creates something positive. Inmates see themselves, by and large as victims, not producers. The real shift then needs to help inmates change from negative producers and victims to positive producers.

Let's take what many of us may consider a typical inmate. Maybe he grew up on the streets of an inner city. Maybe his mom was a crack addict and he didn't know his dad. The only male figures in his life were his mom's boyfriend(s). He went to school and sometime in his adolescence became "too cool for school." He started drinking and or doing drugs and became sexually active. Since his mom moved around a lot, he likely attended multiple schools and before you know it, he was lost in the cracks. By the 9th or 10th grade, he dropped out of school and was getting into serious trouble. To feed his drug habit and to fit in with his "friends" he started burglarizing homes. Stealing anything that wasn't tied down became a way of life and having any girl he sets is eyes on became his passion.

He's now 25 years old and in prison. It took him 25 years to develop those habits. Under the current system, another four or five years in prison will only cement his behaviors in place. When he gets out, he can think of two things, getting high and having as many girls as he can find.

Five years pass and he is now 30. He has violated parole and is back in prison. The trend is clear. He has now spent 30 years learning negative behaviors. I really don't think another five years in prison, under the current system, will do him much good.

I would guess that to effect real change in this guy would take five years or more of concerted, directed effort in which he is a voluntary participant. To make that change, he would have to achieve certain milestones, each of which may take months or years. He would have to be able to try his new behaviors over and over again, failing and succeeding until he gets it right. He would have to be able to, as he changes and makes appropriate progress, pull himself out of the primordial ooze that is the prison's general population and separate himself from the crap. He would need to start living in housing with other individuals who have proven themselves desirous to change. He would have to be given responsibilities and opportunities to succeed and thus fail and succeed again and as long as he shows progress and genuine change, be encouraged to continue. Punishment or setbacks would be inevitable. He would need positive mentors to help him deal with his journey and then he would need to eventually become a mentor to others trying to find their way. This process would require that his guards, over time, learn to trust him and give him responsibility and opportunity to test his new-found life skills realizing that he may fail and need to try again.

This is not a new concept. It is life, one that we live in every day. It is a life of hope, purpose, choice, struggle, and self-selection. It is one that the current prison system does not permit. However, if the UDOC is truly to become a Corrections-type of institution, it is a system and attitude they **must** adopt, at least for those inmates who chose to make the effort to change. The UDOC is in a position to be a perfect "parent" to enact change. They just don't see it.

As mentioned earlier, I don't think for minute that all the inmates in CUCF or any facility would succeed in following such a path. It won't happen. However, implementing a program that allows for some to follow these simple principles would easily shift the recidivism rate from the 70% range to the 40% range. Considering the cost of incarceration to be in the neighborhood of $30,000 per inmate annually, the change would be worth it both in a humanistic sense as well as a financial sense. I am confident such a process is doable within the fences of CUCF.

Chapter 17

The Changing of the Guard

Change is inevitable, Progress is optional.

Tony Robins

About four years into my tenure, dramatic changes came. We received a new warden and deputy warden. A new captain replaced the Programming captain and officers who had been in Education and with whom we had worked closely were all moved to other posts. I found myself having to re-establish important relationships with new people, most of whom were very skeptical of our activities.

The previous officers had witnessed our growth and could easily verify our efforts to create an above board, viable, defendable program. The new officers were extremely skeptical and suspicious of everything we were doing.

In addition to officer changes, chains of command were changed and I found myself having to answer to not just the Programming captain but also to the MEGA captain who saw life from a security only perspective and had little vision or interest in an educational perspective. He was a good guy as I had known him for many years but we saw very few things the same and he showed no confidence in me or CUA/Outreach and our ability to run a good program. He was always very suspicious of all of our activities.

Among the greatest concerns was the current situation with the Inmate Edmond who was largely responsible for Outreach and the developing UPrep program. I had relied on Edmond heavily both for ideas and implementation. Taking the perspective of an inmate who truly wanted to change and provide opportunity for others to change had been critical to our success and was a key element in all we were able to accomplish.

Over the next year however, I came to realize that Corrections was not going to allow an inmate to be my "right hand man" and we determined to replace him with a civilian employee.

I went to the warden and he agreed to allow Edmond to stay on until I could bring in a new Education staff member and have him trained. He agreed, and reminded me that Edmond was to be removed from any Education leadership position.

That spring, I advertised for a new teacher position and set about the process of finding a replacement. In the meantime, most of my efforts went towards defending our program. We were getting pressure from Corrections at every turn. Clearly someone wanted our efforts squashed. From my perspective, the only group that was onboard was the leadership in the various housing units. They remained very supportive. In fact, they started to require more and more involvement by their inmate population and often presented valuable ideas to improve our processes and expand our reach. What had started in STRIVE was spreading in a positive way to some of the other housing units.

Some of the new Education officers started to buy in and we could feel their support as they came to see and understand the good outcomes we were creating. However, others did not and pressure from the captains, etc., was constant.

A short time after that a new sergeant arrived. Because of the other changes we had "received" and negative noises from the rumor mill, I was very worried. Upon his arrival, we had a frank conversation. In a very short time, I found that all my concerns were completely unfounded and I dare say that "Sarge" became our greatest defender and allowed us to go forward despite the many other subtle attacks on our program. He ran interference in our behalf many times;

probably more times than I know. There were many officers who had a positive, supportive influence on the growth and development of CUA/Outreach and UPrep. Sarge was one of the leaders in that category. Without him, it is unlikely that Outreach would have survived or that UPrep would have been built.

As I received applications for our new civilian Outreach Director, I actually had a person in mind I thought would be a great fit. We had several other applicants, one in particular that stood out but I thought my "pick" would work best. However, after the interviews, it was clear that the best candidate was Josh Palmer. He turned out to be a perfect fit and was just what we needed to keep the ball rolling.

After Josh was hired, it took a few weeks to orient him, and we were off and running. It was hard to let Edmond go and I think it was hard for Edmond. This program had been his "baby" and it is never easy to turn over something valuable to someone you don't know. However, Josh filled in and became an outstanding leader and Director of Outreach.

By now, we had a very deep organization. We had turned two of our classrooms into what was referred to as the "Tutor Room." About 20 inmate employees worked on everything from curriculum to Education compliance to computer coding. The Tutor Room also included a printing room where, after their electronic creation, we printed our own text books. It was the "hub" of everything that happened in Education. We were very careful to be completely transparent with the officers and were always looking to implement protocols that would ensure good security and transparency.

Over 8 years, the tutor room grew to create over 80 textbooks for both secondary level courses as well as post-secondary level courses. In the tutor room, they tracked our "Cell Study" program; a program that allowed inmates to work on school in their cells rather than come to the

Education. They tracked Education Compliance of all the inmates in the facility. The tutors supported our testing center and wrote programs that calculated all of our educational information and put it into a useful form. They created and supported our SIS, called InfoNet. Several tutors worked closely with the faculty to provide information and support to provide the best possible services to our students. Mostly, they **loved** to come to work and were some of the best employees I ever worked with. Many of them often worked 50-60-hour weeks. Because they "owned" the processes and outcomes, they were thinking about work all the time. Each of them constantly looked for ways to improve our program.

This is Edmond's perspective during this time:

We became so successful that we started exploring the options to expand our reach to the students who were high school graduates and had high literacy skills. That was the impetus for starting UPrep Academy, a post-secondary Education program. It was our hope that if we started teaching college courses that we would eventually bring the colleges back to the prison. Because of the efforts thrown into UPrep, I stopped my split focus of teaching classes and managing the "tutor room" and gave up facilitating classes. The program had gotten so big that I had to focus solely on managing it. My teaching days were over.

Our student information system (SIS) gave us the ability to report on an individual student in real time, so Corrections began requiring Education to at least the 11th grade level. Failure to do so would result in sanction by the housing unit for being educationally non-compliant. In the beginning this was a tall order for everybody involved. It took a great deal of time and effort to change the hearts and minds of individuals who demanded that we continue a "business as usual" approach. It was a severe learning curve for the inmate population but especially for Corrections. To gain

116

the buy-in of UDC, we wrote policies and procedures outlining every step of the program. To overcome the inmates' distrust of authority, we incentivized the program. Eventually, it became a win/win strategy that brought tremendous results and success.

During our fourth year of success, we had a literal changing of the guard. Every officer involved with building these programs from the beginning was transferred out of Education and assigned to another post. With a new regime, from Deputy Wardens, Captains, Lieutenants, Sergeants and even to the bottom-rung security officers, Principal Mark had his days full with defending our programs and their expansions. Our system of doing things was an absolute culture shock to these seasoned officers. Since they didn't want to understand or assist us in the why and what we were doing, because it was completely foreign to them, it was absolutely impossible to gain their buy-in and support. They began impeding progress and sabotaging our success. They began implementing useless rules that constantly hindered the program.

They created obstacles and restricted the normal inmate movements in and out of the Education corridor. They began limiting the incentives we could offer to the inmate tutors and inmate students alike. Their attitude was as if hell needed to freeze over before they were going to allow inmates to be educated on their watch. No longer was their mission to support the good we were doing; instead, their mission was to stop us. When they realized they couldn't shake our resolve, they began dismantling our team.

After months of defending our work and the individuals who saw the work through, the CUA principal was ordered to terminate me. He called me into his office one mid-morning and with tears in his eyes told me he had to fire me. I wasn't surprised. He and I had had numerous conversations over the years discussing that at some point they weren't going to allow an inmate to be in charge of all

117

the things I was in charge of. Our success and the autonomy he gave me were our "death sentence" so to speak.

Mark identified full well that this was going to happen. As a result, for the past year and a half, we had been delegating my responsibilities to others. We had trained other inmates to assume the many responsibilities Mark had given me. Though we were prepared for this day, that didn't make it any less painful for either of us.

The Principal and I did what we always did when faced with what seemed to be an unsurmountable obstacle. We took 15 minutes to weigh out all the options and possible outcomes. From this we determined two things. First, that the program we had created was vital to the success of the inmate population. Second, that if we were to continue, we would have to protect the program from the UDC. In order to do that, I had to be replaced by a civilian teacher. A civilian staff member would have to be in charge of Outreach and UPrep.

I agreed to train the new teacher but insisted that in so doing, I would be placed on a list of inmates that would not be sent to a county jail through Inmate Placement Program (IPP). I wanted to stay at CUCF, in the STRIVE program and participate in the many UPrep postsecondary classes we had created. I didn't want to be county-ed out.

Mark picked up the phone and called the Deputy Warden to look at the options. The Deputy Warden expressed one stipulation. If he was going to keep me from being county-ed out, he wanted assurance that I would be gone from Education leadership once the new civilian staff was trained. He agreed to the terms.

When Mark told me of the stipulation, I was certain that the Deputy Warden wouldn't keep his word. When the time came, I would find myself on a transport van headed to some god-forsaken county jail. Principal Mark, being the man, he is, defended the Deputy Warden and said that he believed the Deputy Warden to be a good man and that he would keep his word. In complete disagreement I responded, "Only time will tell."

Truth be told, I knew that I was no longer in a position to negotiate. Even without this agreement, I would have stayed on to train the new teacher. What we had created was too important not to. If CUA/Outreach and UPrep had a chance at surviving, I had to get out of the way and let a civilian come in and do my job. I was certain of that.

The Principal took the next couple months advertising and establishing a list of candidates for the new job. In that search, he found the perfect match. At the beginning of the next school year, I began training the new Outreach Director. The transition was swift and fairly smooth. There were a handful of hurdles created mostly by my own ego. I found it hard to let it go. It was my "baby" and I was very passionate about the program and its success. Slowly but surely, I took steps back to allow the new director to find his own path. It was one of the hardest things I have ever had to do. The fact that the new director was a perfect fit made it easier. I would like to think that I turned it all over rather gracefully.

During the transition period, the principal was told that he had to reduce my pay back down to 40 cents per hour. That meant a significant pay cut for me, about $145 each month. I took the pay cut in stride but it was wearing on me. Several things were happening that added to my frustrations. I had applied for a UCI (Utah Correctional Industries) position in the Sign Shop. However, I was not given an interview. I also tried to enroll in the Snow College Building Trades program and was hoping I could move up to be a tutor there. However, the Programming lieutenant wouldn't approve my application. The principal went out of his way to meet these individuals personally but to no avail. It was clear to both of us that I was being blackballed.

In the end, I finished training the new teacher without incident and was then removed from the tutor room and

119

placed at a desk in the copy center. Mark allowed me to stay on as long as I would fly under the radar. I continued to send out applications for other work opportunities throughout CUCF.

My new role became just that. I kept writing curriculum for a UPrep Spanish course and each week I would reapply for work outside Education. OMR would approve my applications but I would never be called for an interview. I felt like I was the most qualified person never to be interviewed, let alone hired.

UDC seemed to accept my new existence in the copy room. After all, I was completely removed from the mix and spent my days developing a Spanish curriculum. How much harm could I be? My experience as an educational tutor taught me that the best way to learn something was to teach it. I therefore decided to master Spanish by creating a curriculum and teach it. Learning Spanish had been one of my first goals upon being incarcerated. Now I had the time to really give myself to it.

After a couple of months of a lower pay, I asked the principal if he would restore my previous salary. I was hemorrhaging money and figured after four and a half years of service to the facility and owing to the fact that CUCF wouldn't let me move on to another job, I had the right to cover my monthly expenses, at least that was my thinking.

I asked Mark for the change. He told me that though he agreed with my thinking, once the Warden sees the change, I would be immediately IPP'd out to county. I asked him to go ahead with the change. Within a week, I was on my way to Daggett County Jail.

Chapter 18

HOPE? – Nope!

Even in the inevitable moments when all seems hopeless,
men know that without hope they cannot really live,
and in agonizing desperation they cry for the bread
of hope.

Martin Luther King Jr

This chapter was written in May of 2019. It may be the case that this and other programs within the UDC have been modified/improved to be more effective. As of this date, this information is consistent with current activities.

I would like to start this section with the same comments about the good nature of the officers I work with in CUCF. I believe they are good people trapped in a broken system. With that in mind, I would like to give a quick narrative about the Helping Offenders Parole Effectively (HOPE) program. It is a residential substance abuse treatment program contained in the Fir housing unit inside CUCF. The folks here are very proud of the program. The director is a good man who is doing all he can to implement and execute a quality program. The idea of residential treatment programs is well founded and proven to be effective. It is the model used in most programs on the street. However, inside the prison, there are some real issues.

To outline the program, it consists of a system in which individuals who have been through the program mentor and support those that are newer in the process. There are senior and junior mentors. There are several different levels. There are certain requirements by individuals and by specific sections. All of this sounds perfect to me. The process is based on the idea of individual buy-in and individual progress.

Participants must work to improve themselves and also help others do the same. Senior mentors are responsible for their group of participants including reporting non-compliance to the OMR and holding individuals accountable for their behavior. Security staff teach classes on all kinds of topics. The curriculum, as I have had opportunity to see it, looks like it is well-designed and written. The courses cover topics like Impact of Crime, Parenting Basics and Tobacco Recovery. They have a set of core values that are spot-on and an outline of unacceptable character defects that define acceptable behavior. Their participant handbook is 140 pages of well-defined, outlined expectations and processes. Looking at the program outline and processes, it is exactly what needs to happen. However, the existing program is heavy-handed and lacks any type of positive incentive. In addition, the whole process is almost completely corrupt. Let me explain:

Over the years, as I have visited with many of the inmates who have participated in the HOPE program, every single one has told me the same story. They tell tales of staff members not teaching, faking testing outcomes, contracted disciplinary processes and the most drug use inside CUCF. Let me go into a little detail:

A senior mentor, who is an inmate, is responsible for his group, about 50 inmates. Each inmate has a level. Senior mentors are responsible for reporting bad behavior and each senior mentor has a quota of required reportings. Each member of the community likewise is required to turn in a certain number of infractions. Each has a quota of violations reporting. Failure to do so results in sanctions by the OMR. However, the current prisoner code dictates that doing so constitutes a "rat" and results in retaliation by other inmates. Inmates cannot turn in other inmates. They will get beaten.

As a result, most reported infractions or "pull-ups" as they are called, are made up and contracted. Inmates who have been through the program often speak of buying or contracting pull-ups on other inmates for an $8 box of coffee or a carton of dried eggs. That will buy enough pull-ups for a month. They all say it is well worth it. One inmate will allow another inmate to fabricate an infraction and report it as a pull-up for a price.

In other words, each week the senior mentor reports to OMR. There he describes the pull-ups that happened in his section for the previous week as well as the consequences of those pull-ups. These pull-ups come from individual inmates who were paid off with coffee, eggs or other commodities for the "privilege" of receiving a pull-up. Since too many pull-ups for the same infraction results in a visit to OMR, inmates are careful to ensure their pull-ups are for different infractions. Since nearly all the inmates in the program are required to give pull-ups, the contract process ensures that inmates will comply with the OMR/HOPE requirements while never really getting in trouble. This corrupt system has been in place for at least as long as I worked at CUCF.

Another part of the problem is found with some of the staff. HOPE has a series of courses that are taught by Corrections staff, at least they are supposed to be the instructors. Each course is monitored by testing. At the beginning of the course, the inmate takes a pretest. They participate in the course and then at the end, they take a post-test. Adequate progress is required to receive credit. The inmate/students come to class and on the first day are told by the inmate tutors to do poorly on the pretest. The staff instructor is nearly always absent. During the course, rather than study appropriate materials, they watch movies, sit and shoot the breeze or both. Periodically, the staff member sticks his head in to say hi. At the end of the course, the inmate tutors provide the answers to the test and then administer the post-test, thus ensuring all participants get above 80%. Nothing is taught, nothing is learned, and there is no behavior that is changed. Inmates game the system and Corrections has made no effort to "correct" the problem.

Statements made to me by inmates who were former participants include:

"It costs me a box of coffee, $8 a month to have my contracts taken care of. Best $8 I ever spent."

"If an honest individual goes into the HOPE program, they will come out a liar because there is no other way to survive the system."

"I try to stay as far away from HOPE as I can."

"Not a single class I took in HOPE was valid."

"Nothing good goes on in HOPE." "There are more drugs in Fir than in any other part of the prison."

"There are constant fights, tension and problems in Fir (the housing unit where HOPE is located), more than in any other housing unit I've lived in."

It is important to note that these things were told me with no ulterior motive. I asked, they answered. The only feeling I got from them is that they wished that the program ran as designed so they could have received a benefit. I believe that if HOPE were fixed, there are many inmates that would want to participate receiving the help, growth and support it could provide.

I don't believe the director of HOPE, who is a good person, has any idea this is going on. I don't know how many of his staff know about it. I only know that, though the idea and intent is very good, corruption is rampant and nothing good comes of it.

I have heard the same types of stories about Conquest, a similar program inside the Draper Prison site, but I have done no inquiry into it.

It is a shame because, if done correctly, these environments are exactly what are needed to create real change on the inside so that change can occur on the outside. If a Tier program were to be instigated, many of the same processes as are in HOPE would be enacted. However, the monitoring would be real, the effectiveness would be ensured and focus would be to help inmates help themselves in a good way. They would have to employ the trust but verify methods we used in Education as well as different incentives as motivation. In addition, it has to be voluntary and look to identify and help individuals who have "...come to themselves."

As I see it, the problem lies in several areas. First of all, the inmate leaders are not scrutinized, qualified, and held accountable. Second, there seems to be little buy-in by staff. Absentee teaching and supervision is a real problem. Third, there is no oversight by administration. This has gone on for eight or more years. Finally, there is a definite culture problem that is evident in all of this, part of a much larger "us vs them" culture throughout the entire prison system. Currently, there is no HOPE.

To understand the perspective of inmates, we quote from two previously cited offenders. The first is an article written by Brian Wood for the *Ogden Standard-Examiner*. It is the inmate's perspective of the HOPE program.

I have recently completed the HOPE program at Central Utah Correctional Facility in Gunnison, Utah. The majority of the prison's drug offenders are placed in this residential substance abuse treatment program for one year during their incarceration. They are presented with classes, counseling, increased rules and staff, extra amenities, and many other things.

I understand the program is funded by the federal government as part of the war on drugs. The prison receives money for each prisoner sent through the program. The goal being to reduce recidivism, or the likelihood a prisoner will be sent back to prison after being released. HOPE stands for Helping Offenders Parole Effectively.

I entered the program with an open mind and a positive attitude. Let me first say I believe many prisoners need help in the form of substance abuse treatment and I believe the HOPE program was an honest attempt at a solution, at least in the beginning. Unfortunately there are some realities of prison that make it impossible for HOPE to function as it was intended.

The HOPE program is based on the Therapeutic Community (TC) model. The fundamental idea is that community members hold other members accountable for their actions; meaning, prisoners are encouraged to tell on each other. I found a couple of problems with this.

Problem #1: Prisoners don't tell on one another, because it's dangerous. Prison culture is not about to change for the rules of a program. Being a "rat" is the quickest way for an inmate to become the target of violence in prison. If there's one thing prisoners are, it is patient, and if there's more things, it's often a combination of being unscrupulous, mentally ill, and violent. These are not the characteristics of individuals you want to make your enemy.

Problem #2: The HOPE program is made up of individuals who are being forced to participate. This creates a mentality to fight tooth and nail against every aspect of the program, making a healthy therapeutic community impossible. Perhaps the TC model could work in a prison environment if the community was made up of volunteers, but the current recruiting method insures it will remain broken.

The idea, I imagine, in being willing to tell on other inmates is to see if you will completely change your way of thinking from the criminal perspective. Unfortunately, it doesn't work like that. In my entire year of being in the program I never saw a single prisoner use "the process" (telling on someone) in a therapeutically intentional fashion. I have only seen prisoners use the process as a weapon to manipulate, or for their own gain.

126

The program entices prisoners to become snitches using financial incentives and offering additional privileges. This usually appeals to the most short-sighted and instant-gratification-seeking individuals (typical drug addict flaws). They trade their own safety for power, money, and privileges. This trade feeds into their anti-social personalities and manipulative and selfish tendencies. Prisoners who choose this path cannot return to general population for obvious reasons, but they are few.

So how does it work if a prisoner is unable to follow the rules of HOPE without great risk to personal safety? They don't need to because everything is faked. Prisoners go through the motions of "the process," fill out the necessary reports and accept consequences, but it's a charade. Staff knows this but there's really nothing they can do about it and probably don't care to. They just play along.

I just don't understand putting forth all the effort to continue the lie when everyone involved knows what's really going on. Why not find a different program or model? If the broken TC model were the only problem, I'm sure I would have looked right past that and focused on the good, but that's not the only part of the program being faked. When a prisoner graduates HOPE, the claim is that prisoner has been given the tools to stay sober and succeed in regular society. Most of this learning and development is supposed to occur in the first 4 months in what is called "Intensive." My Intensive schedule was a mix of inmate- and officer-led classes. The classes have names like "Stress Management," "Relapse Prevention," "Anger Management," "Conflict Resolution," Overcoming Addiction," and other catchy titles. I imagine funding (your tax dollars) is secured by pitching this wonderful bouquet of personal growth and recovery courses provided to offenders, especially when a licensed state employee is facilitating the courses.

The inmate-led classes consisted of us sitting at the tables in our section and looking busy. We often did this for 5-6 hours per day. On days when state employees actually held their scheduled class, which was only about half the time, the instructor would often come in, turn on a movie and leave. I can't recall being taught anything except on the last couple days of classes each term. This was when we would go over the test questions and answers, so that we could all pass the tests. It was a huge show.

I do think the writing assignments were a positive thing. These assignments had prisoners focus on the negative impact drug use had on them and the people close to them. Prisoners also had to identify potential obstacles in their future and create plans for dealing with those things. If there is a redeeming aspect to the program this would be it; however, my personal experience has led me to the following conclusions. The HOPE program cannot function the way it was intended in a prison environment as long as its community members are being forced to participate. The vast majority of the HOPE program was a colossal waste of my time and an even greater waste of tax-payer money.

This isn't the first time I have witnessed taxpayers being defrauded by a government entity, but it is the first time I've felt like blowing the whistle, and it has nothing to do with our legislature being duped and wasting a ton of money. The real tragedy is the men who may have been saved had they really been proffered tools that would help them stay sober and be successful. It seems like every week I am hearing about a HOPE graduate coming right back to prison or dying from a drug overdose. The prison is not responsible for the action of these men, but I wonder, if offenders were actually receiving the treatment being purported and paid for, maybe some of these men might have gone on to live productive lives, or just lived, period.

I might add that when Brian wrote this article he told me that he was invited to the Executive Director's office to discuss the issue. According to Brian, the Executive Director seemed more interested in justifying the current

128

system rather than identifying the problems and fixing them. HOPE comes with a large federal grant. Not losing that money as opposed to resolving the real issues seemed to be the focus.

Rather than rely on one witness, here is the perspective provided by Inmate Edmond. He contrasts STRIVE and HOPE. STRIVE is a completely unfunded program initiated by the Gale housing unit Captain and her staff some years ago. HOPE is a funded and legislative-mandated substance abuse program.

CUCF facilitates two programs in their facility. One is a completely voluntary program called STRIVE (Strength Through Responsibility, Integrity, Values and Effort). The program is part of the GALE housing unit. It is self-regulating and has a minimal amount of officer involvement (unless you get into trouble). There are five levels (0-4) of attainment and as you increase your levels, your incentives increase. To participate you had to leave your convict mentality at the door, maintain a 40-hour productive weekly schedule and adhere to the facility rules without exception. Part of the 40 -hour productive schedule required you to take at least five STRIVE classes. The classes focused on everything from thinking and behavior modification to crochet to various building trades and occupational career options. All classes were facilitated by like-minded inmates who took pride in the classes they taught. They required a one-year commitment by which time an inmate could achieve the level-4 status. At that point, you could stay as long as you like as long as you followed the rules, were willing to facilitate classes and were willing to mentor and support the new participants. Once in STRIVE, most inmates stayed in GALE even after completing the program. The STRIVE captain at the time claimed that 90% of inmates that parole from STRIVE didn't come back. That's a 10% recidivism rate compared with a statewide 70% rate.

129

The other CUCF program is the HOPE program. It is part of the FIR housing unit. HOPE (Helping Offenders Parolee Effectively) is a therapeutic community focused on substance abuse. To participate you must be mapped for substance abuse treatment as part of your case action plan. My guess is that you got mapped for HOPE when you answered yes to the "have you ever used illicit drugs" question back in R&O. Either that or substance abuse was an element of your crime. The program is heavy-handed with rules, sanctions and heavy officer involvement and offers few incentives. The sections are governed by inmates who have been assigned by the licensed substance abuse counselor (LSAC) to be crew bosses often referred to as Junior or Senior Mentors. There are six steps to the program with steps four, five and six reserved for graduates who stay in the program as leadership.

There are two phases to the HOPE program. The first phase, called Intensive, lasts for about sixteen weeks. During this four-month period, new members are sequestered and required to stay within the housing unit to participate as a group in core Programming classes, physical exercise and activities and attend all section meetings. These classes and activities are held Monday through Friday from 5:30 am until 4:00 pm and are usually 45 minutes long with 15-minute breaks

Phase two of the program is comprised of a required 40-hour productive schedule that must include Programming and Education classes or employment outside the Fir housing unit. About two months before graduation, an inmate is required to attend weekly phase two group and individual therapy sessions with a HOPE therapist. The group sessions have anywhere from eight to twelve inmates and last about an hour. The individual session are about 30-40 minutes depending on the individual's effort and participation.

The main emphasis of the HOPE program is accountability. This is largely achieved by calling out your peers when they have a mishap or are in direct violation of the program or facility rules. Depending on the infraction you are given a "call" or a "pull-up" or a "Tribunal." Calls and Pull-ups are typically followed up by a "table" process and tribunals require that you stand in front of the entire section of inmates while being asked questions about your behavior by each member of your crew. After answering all their questions, the scolding portion of the tribunal begins. Typically your entire crew and the section leadership will give you feedback on your behavior. Sometimes other members of the section will also give feedback.

Once this is done you are told to stand out in the mini-yard while your crew members and leadership talk about you and decide your sanctions. Tribunals usually result in a no-tolerance probation period of 30 to 60 days with a bunch of community service hours or Remedial Reform Group (RRG) which requires a whole new level of Programming participation by the individual. While on RRG, your progression through the program stops. You are required to spend three hours each morning performing community service and must sit alone the rest of the day and write in your journal. You cannot talk with anyone other than your crew boss and are restricted from purchasing or consuming commissary food items. Your journal entries are reviewed by the HOPE therapist and you receive weekly feedback through the RRG group therapy sessions. You are placed on RRG for up to 60 days depending on the seriousness of the infraction and the number of times you have previously been placed on RRG.

Another measure of accountability in HOPE is through a dozen or so writing assignments. As you advance through the program the assignments become more thought-provoking and require more and more personal accountability. Most assignments are focused on your past

131

life struggles with relationships and substance abuse and are required to be read out loud in front of your peers. After reading your assignment to the section, leadership and the LSAC give their feedback and then decide if you followed the assignment syllabus and whether you pass or have to complete an add-on or perhaps a complete re-write.

The HOPE program, though well-intended, was completely ineffective for most participants for several reasons. First, the program was mandatory. Forced participation under such personal circumstances created huge amounts of animosity. Second, the program was mostly corrupt. Most pull-ups and calls were contracted and thus staged. None of the required courses were truly taught.

The inmates at CUCF all had similar opinions about both the STRIVE and HOPE programs. STRIVE was encouraged by anyone who was really focused on being a better person. This included murderers, drug addicts, gang bangers and sex offenders alike. The only inmates who opposed the STRIVE program were inmates who simply refused to change and prided themselves on being a convict. Despite the diversity of offenders within the Gale housing unit, STRIVE had a reputation of being the most peaceful, get-along housing unit in the prison system.

From the perspective of most inmates, STRIVE was a desired program for any inmate who looked to change his course. HOPE, on the other hand, was considered a farce and a sham and hated by literally every inmate within CUCF. Interestingly, STRIVE was a program created by an innovative captain and her staff. No money. No additional resources. HOPE is a mandated program with big dollars attached. Corrections hangs on to HOPE with a tight hold and often marginalizes STRIVE.

Living in general population in CUCF wasn't bad. As long as you followed the rules, you could pretty much come and go as you wanted to. Movement times were at the top of every hour. You could attend classes in Programming or

Education or you could sit around your section watching TV or playing games. Yard was twice a day in the winter and three times a day in the summer. You could isolate yourself in your cell or you could hang out in the day room. No one was going to force you to reform or rehabilitate. You were solely responsible for any change you wanted to make in yourself. Unfortunately, doing this kind of time is a waste of time in my mind. The majority of offenders in general population are hard cases. The most severe convicts. For me, they weren't pleasant to be around. So, I applied to go to the STRIVE program.

I was in STRIVE for six months before having to go to HOPE. During that time I had completed my high school diploma and in fact was asked by the faculty at CUA to be a graduate speaker at graduation. I had also earned my second STRIVE level which allowed me to buy a decent pair of shoes. I spent my days going to Programming and Education classes while making sure that I made time for my five required STRIVE classes. I pretty much kept a 60-hour productive week. I learned to crochet, read music, trade stocks on the financial markets and started studying Spanish. I exercised every day and ran my first marathon. (That's a lot of laps around the exercise yard). Everybody around me was mostly encouraging and positive. STRIVE contained a vast amount of knowledge. My peers were all working towards self-improvement and were willing to share their previous positive experiences with me and anyone else who had shown an interest. The same sharing occurred in other housing units but the previous experiences and teaching shared were negative and criminal. My time in STRIVE was likely the most productive time I spent while incarcerated. No one was drinking, drugging or strong arming anyone else. Everyone for the most part followed the rules and was amicable. The tension was extremely low and the place was fairly stress free. Even the guards had a different persona. They were helpful, kind, compassionate, and respectful.

STRIVE felt more like a reformatory rather than a prison. There was camaraderie like nothing I had ever experienced before or since.

Moving to the Fir housing unit and the HOPE program was a severe culture shock. I had to make a lot of adjustments that caused my rehabilitation to be in regression. There was tremendous amount of internal politics to navigate, something that hadn't existed in STRIVE. The incredible amount of backbiting and tension had a very unproductive effect on my goals. There was no unity and everybody was overly concerned about everybody else. There was constant bullying and targeting. The guards seemed to lack humanity and appeared to be in on the chaos. I was confused about how this program was going to help me become a better person.

After being in the program for a week, the director tried kicking me out because I was on a five- to-life sentence and it would be another two and a half years before I would see the Parole Board (BOPP). Apparently, he didn't see the importance of starting my rehabilitation sooner rather than later. To him, I was taking up the spot of someone who would be released much sooner. I appealed to the lieutenant. He said that he would keep me for another week while I appealed the decision in front of the weekly OMR (Offender Management Review).

Attending OMR was intimidating. More than a dozen staff attended, including the deputy warden, the housing unit captain, the lieutenant, and sergeants. All the caseworkers, the LSACs and HOPE therapists and, of course, the Director of HOPE, also attended. I stood my ground and made a case for why I should be allowed to stay in the program. I explained how important it was for me to get a handle on my anger issues and to take accountability for everything I had done. I made sure they knew I was committed to my rehabilitation and that I would take every aspect of the program seriously. I must have been pretty convincing because they decided to make an exception and allowed me to stay. I think in truth, however, is that I got to stay because I was the first inmate to ever enter OMR and declare that he wanted to stay in the program. I had to make the same plea several months later.

Within the first week, all of the new arrivals are called to the OMR room for an orientation and to sign their HOPE contracts. One of the LSACs explained how the program worked and told everybody in attendance that the program was completely voluntary. After her spiel, she asked if there was anyone who didn't want to volunteer to participate. One guy raised his hand and said he didn't. She asked him a couple of questions and then told everybody to hang tight while she excused herself. When she came back in she brought three additional officers with her. She then ordered the inmate to stand up and face the wall. After he complied, the three officers surrounded him and placed handcuffs on him. He was then escorted out and sent to E-level, which is a 23-hour lockdown section. After they left the OMR, the lady asked, with a smile on her face, if there was anyone else who would like to opt out. I sat there amazed at the theatrics of the entire situation.

It didn't take long for me to understand why every inmate in CUCF thought the HOPE program was a farce. My experience was that Intensive was a huge waste of time. I had the opportunity of taking most of the core Programming classes prior to becoming part of the HOPE program. I was actually looking forward to retaking them until I sat in on the HOPE version. Each class was facilitated by an inmate. Once class started, the facilitator would take roll then would begin writing all the answers to the upcoming post-test up on the board for everyone to copy. It was seven weeks of copying answers for about 15 minutes and then sitting around for another 30 minutes bored to tears. The whole thing was a huge sham. None of the actual material was covered. Classes that had video content were usually muted as the program aired so everyone could sit around and bullshit with each other. Never once did the LSAC sit in on a class to make certain the intended purpose was preserved. Everybody was in on it.

They called the process of holding others accountable for their behavior, "using the process." Each person was required to use the process at least twice a week. This meant that you were required to address another person's behavior when you witnessed an infraction. Otherwise you could be held for "standing in silence" which was a pull-up which came with 50 hours of community service.

By design, one would think that this method of accountability would cause everyone to rise to the occasion. It is a similar method used by Nazi Germany in the 1930's. Well, it didn't work. Instead, I'm thoroughly convinced that it created better manipulators. It was standard practice to find a couple of guys and contract calls and pull-ups with them each week. If you agreed to let them make a call or pull-up on you this week, you got to make a call on them the next week. Make this arrangement with a handful of guys and you would never have to make a legitimate call. If you chose not to go along then you became a target so that everyone was watching everything you did and "calling you out" as it were. The only other time I would witness a legitimate call was when two individuals got sideways with one another and started fighting.

There were a few beneficial parts of HOPE that actually helped. You could call an individual "to the table" and discuss a problem. It was a great way to heighten someone's awareness of a particular behavior without invoking a consequence. Tables were facilitated by two members of leadership. Both parties would be called and the person calling the table would explain to the other party why he had brought him to the table. Once he was done, he would have to sit silently as the other party gave his rebuttal. This would go back and forth until both parties were satisfied. After which the peer mentors would give their feedback. The two participants weren't allowed to respond at that point.

It was quite a ritual. However, I discovered the value of communicating in this way; to listen and assess without interrupting. I learned to be patient and assess everything they would say until they were finished. Then I would sit quietly for a moment and formulate my response in a way that was accountable, non-aggressive and non-challenging. It taught me to be respectful of a person with a different point of view.

Besides the therapy sessions that I will describe later, the "table" process and the written assignments were the only two good things about HOPE. The written assignments helped me dig deeper and deeper into my emotions while being accountable for my behavior. They helped me to uncover some of the reasons I committed the crimes that brought me to prison. I took a lot of pride in completing these assignments and spent a great deal of time reworking them. I felt that in the end it would be the one valuable thing I could take from HOPE.

In HOPE, there was a tremendous amount of pressure to cheat and use someone else's copied assignments. That was the regular practice of most participants. They would change the names but the stories would remain the same. As a junior mentor I probably heard every single assignment repeated at least a dozen times. It never made sense to me that the LSAC didn't detect this behavior. It was apparent to me so I figured either he was in on it or he just didn't care. I also thought it was odd when someone had to have someone read their assignment for them because they were too illiterate to read their own handwriting. Why didn't the LSAC have something to say about that? All in all, I kept these thoughts to myself. I was already being shunned by nearly everyone since I chose to do my own work. The logic I was surrounded by was that if you aren't with us then you must be against us.

The phase-two group therapy sessions were a waste of time as well. No one, including me, wanted to be there. We were all within two months of completion and just wanted to move on. No real work was being done during this process. On your final group your peers would vote on a scale of 1-5 on whether or not you would relapse and/or return to prison. 5 was the best score possible and suggested that you wouldn't have any problems re-entering society and maintaining your sobriety. In my mind, most of the guys in the program deserved a 1, maybe a 2. Yet we all sat around and handed out 5's like we were all cured of all our personal issues. It was absurd.

The one-on-one individual therapy sessions with my HOPE therapist is where the real work began for me. In eight 45-minute sessions I felt I was beginning to make headway on why I had acted out in such a violent way when I got angry. In my first session the therapist asked why I used substances and I told him, "I don't. I use anger."

When he asked me to clarify I said, "I was addicted to anger long before I ever started drinking or using cocaine." I found that when I got angry people got out of the way and left me alone. He wanted to know how I felt about that and I responded, "It makes me feel full of shame, guilt, and remorse."

"I hate that I have destroyed my life and abandoned my children." And, "There has got to be a better way." Then he said something profound.

He said, "Good, I think we can work with that."

"Just so you know, I will have very few answers for you but if you allow me to walk this journey with you then you will likely find your own answers along the way."

I was immediately impressed and got to work. It was an extremely effective part of my incarceration. Just as I was feeling that I was getting somewhere, I had completed my eight sessions and was granted a successful completion certificate and I was a HOPE graduate.

The problem was that I was just getting started. Leaving HOPE and going to a different housing unit meant that I would no longer have access to the therapist. I decide to return to OMR and once again plead my case. I had been to OMR a dozen times or so. Everyone knew me by name and had interacted with me in one way or another. I had everyone's support except the HOPE director's. His argument was that if he provided aftercare for me that he would have to provide it for everyone else. My rebuttal was to state the obvious: "No one else wants to spend a single day in this program after graduation unless they are part of leadership. Of those who do stay, how many have ever asked for more therapy sessions?"

They were worrying about something that didn't exist. There was no demand for it. Anyway, my question got their attention. I was asked to leave. A short time later my therapist called me in his office and said he had been given permission to treat me once a month until I left HOPE.

I asked him if it was possible to get anything done in so short a time being spread so far apart.

He said, "No, and that is why I want you to be here every Friday."

"As far as anybody is concerned, I'm only seeing you once a month. Will that be ok with you?"

I smiled and thanked him. It seems he could see in me a viable, workable student/patient. For the first time I felt like I had an ally.

We spent the next 10 months or so every Friday for several hours getting to the bottom of what ailed me. I had countless breakthroughs and just as many epiphanies. I was beginning to heal from my tumultuous childhood. I was overcoming all the mental, physical, and sexual abuse I received as a child. For the first time in my life someone was willing to listen without judgement and assumption. I got to tell my story, in my words, completely unedited. The process brought me to forgiveness as I began to understand my parent's limitations. I learned to trust those who I loved and who had supported me.

I became accountable for the crap that was mine and learned to let go of the crap that wasn't. The experience has forever changed my life. I know that I am a better person, husband, father and friend because of it. I will always be grateful for this very unique opportunity. I will also be always grateful for the man who willingly walked with me to help uncover my darkest demons.

Our sessions ended after 10 months because my therapist shared some of his cookies with a couple inmates. Apparently, this is against policy and procedure so they forced him into retirement. I had a couple more sessions with him before he had to go. On the last session I took the opportunity to make sure that he knew the impact he had on me and how grateful I was for his help. His response was very modest. He said, "Edmond, you did all the work. I was just along for the ride. You make sure you take care of yourself, my friend." With tears in our eyes, I shook his hand and gave him a hug. He was the first person in Corrections to ever call me by my first name and shake my hand. He's the only person in Corrections I ever hugged.

I remained in the HOPE program for another year. In total I spent three years in the Fir. After my graduation from HOPE, I transferred to an inactive section of Fir that housed inmates before and after the program. Shortly after that, I moved to Gale and restarted the STRIVE program from which I received a certificate.

Although very little good goes on in HOPE, thanks to my access to therapy, and the professional therapy I received, it was invaluable to me.

Chapter 19

IPP – The Tail Wagging the Dog

Don't put the cart before the horse.
John Heywood

This is the part of this book that will cause the most grief to the powers that be. I therefore pre-apologize. IPP stands for Inmate Placement Program. It has a nice ring to it and sounds like something that has obvious benefit for inmates. NOT! It is The Tail Wagging the Dog.

IPP is the most loathed piece of the Utah Department of Corrections. Though noble in intention, it is the antithesis to reducing recidivism. As it has been explained to me, the Governor worked with the sheriffs of many of the counties in the state to find a way to fund their respective local jails. Most rural counties in Utah don't have the tax base to pay for a decent jail facility. Not too long ago, they were rundown hellholes, for lack of a better way to express it.

Working together, the state and local counties devised a plan whereby the state would provide inmates to the various county jails and would pay the jails to house said inmates. In return, the jails agreed to provide the same services for inmate education as the prisons are supposed to. When I suggested the latter part of the agreement to the Executive Director of the UDC, he was not sure that is the case. Anyway, it all sounds great, right?

NOT!

IPP is the antithesis to reducing recidivism. It is also the sacred cow of the Utah State Department of Corrections. It is the tail that constantly wags the dog.

Mention IPP to an inmate who is a KQ5 (which means he has a good prison record), is healthy, is being productive as a worker, volunteer, and or student and also has less than 3 years to the gate and he will shudder. Imagine living in Russia during the cold war. You are constantly looking over your shoulder worrying that you will be put on "the list." From experience, you know full well that it is not uncommon for someone who is on "the list" to disappear. Every day you fear being sent to Siberia. IPP has become the punishment for being a model inmate.

As the name implies, IPP has complete control of where inmates are housed. Odds are that if an inmate fits the description above and has no mental or physical health issues, they will be on "the list" to be "rolled up." These inmates are often the most productive inmates in CUCF. They are often the ones who are trying to overcome the system and trying to change their lives. They often work in Education or Programming or outside maintenance. They are making something better of themselves. They very often serve as volunteers in the various productive programs in the facility. Often, they are part of the STRIVE program in the Gale housing unit.

When they are IPP'd out or "rolled up" they go from something productive and useful in CUCF to a cell in some county jail with little or no yard, little or no educational opportunities, and little to no job opportunities. They sit all day and hear the local short-timers brag of their criminal exploits. They go from a life they selected by their positive actions to living in a proverbial sewer. Though there are several exceptions, most county jails are not set up for long-term inmate correction. The IPP system is such that if you try to improve and get along and make yourself better, you are punished.

Some jails do a very good job of providing opportunity for change. I have visited many of them and it is easy to identify those that "get it." In addition, I have visited with all the Education personnel who work in the county jails around the state. It is clear which ones "get it" and which ones don't. I worked closely with those who are interested in providing a real opportunity for inmate. The Education staff in most jails want to provide something of value but often run into the road blocks of nonexistent facilities or an uncooperative jail commander. Most jails are like that.

One of many examples of this is Don. He was an integral part of our Education tutor room. He was sent to county 6 months before my retirement. When I first met Don, as I outlined earlier, he had a criminal mentality. Over the course of several years, as he worked in the Education department, he evolved into the person he wanted to be. He came to himself and was no longer fit for prison. Now he remains in a county jail with nothing to do but read books, play cards and listen to ugly stories. It is sad. I can only hope that the progress he has made isn't lost. I made multiple requests to have him returned to CUCF. He will languish in the county jail.

I am told that IPP is a problem that cannot be fixed. However, I believe that if people would take a real look at the situation, it could be fixed and, in fact, be a major asset in reducing recidivism. It would not be difficult, with a few modifications, to integrate IPP into a Tiered system of inmate rehabilitation. Let me outline a possible scenario.

In the "A Real Solution" chapter of this book you will get an outline of the potentially successful process. County jails could be modified to accommodate any level of tiered inmates, Tier 3 through Tier 6. They would have to create programs that accommodate the activities of and progress levels of inmate in their specific tier. For example, a county jail could start a cabinet shop in which they teach cabinet making skills. That would be a Tier 6 activity. If the program operated correctly, that jail would look to attract Tier 6 inmates who had a desire to learn cabinet making. The jail would have to prove they could provide the service. Any participating inmates would have to qualify through their progression through the Tier system. In addition, through

JRI (Justice Reform Initiative), participating inmates could, through successful completion, earn the opportunity for an earlier parole.

Some time ago, there was a county jail that ran a cabinet shop for a while. It was not successful for one major reason. The inmates they selected had not changed. They were still criminals. When they got to the jail facility and found a new level of freedom, some of them continued in their criminal behavior. Thus the program failed.

If, on the other hand, only inmates who, though the self-selection process had, over an extended period of time, proven that they were changing and becoming better people, had been allowed in the program, I believe the program would have been successful.

Perhaps a specific county jail wants to provide an SOTP program or a DOTP program. There are several that currently do and one in particular that does an outstanding job of it. Those programs would attract Tier 4 and 5 inmates who need those programs in their progression.

Other jails may choose not to create programs that fit in the Tier system. They could house those inmates who choose not to seek for parole or those who have tried the Tier system and continually fail. In those cases, adding an exterior fence, and a tower to the jail facility would be fairly inexpensive, would increase their security and allow them to take those inmates who want to remain thugs.

Imagine county supervisors meeting with local industry owners and contracting and teaching inmates to help them do their work. State resources could help coordinate and create what industries have the greatest local need for labor. Local industries would not feel undermined but assisted by inmate labor, increasing their bottom line.

Some argue that these ideas cost money and wouldn't be feasible. My argument is that they would save millions of dollars by reducing recidivism, would provide a much better bang for the taxpayers' dollar and would be the right thing to do for the inmate who needs help. It would likewise protect the citizenry that will someday have these men as neighbors.

I think our current governor is a good person. I have heard him speak several times and see our state as being very healthy as a result of his quality leadership. That is to his credit. I believe the same thing about the lieutenant governor. They are good people. They have made commitments and promises and they work hard for the State of Utah. I believe that the governor's office, if they could see the options available, would readily jump onboard and want to do the right thing. No one has helped them see the picture of what is possible.

Using the county jails as a valued part of a Tiered progressive system would make them a huge asset in reducing recidivism.

This is the experience of Inmate Edmond and the county jail system. His narrative makes an accurate description of what is the IPP process. It is a continuation of his story in the chapter, "The Changing of the Guard."

Much of the following narrative covers over three years' time. However, it all relates to the mess that is IPP and thus is included in this chapter.

After a couple of months of a lower pay, I asked the Principal if he would restore my previous salary. I was hemorrhaging money and figured after four and a half years of service to the facility and owing to the fact that CUCF wouldn't let me move on to another job, I had the right to cover my monthly expenses, at least that was my thinking.

I asked Mark for the change. He told me that though he agreed with my thinking, once the Warden sees the change, I would be immediately IPP'd out to county. I asked him to go ahead with the change. Within a week, I was on my way to Daggett County Jail.

145

Daggett County Jail – the Beginning of the End

Before leaving CUCF I was taken down to the IPP property matrix. With the exception of a handful of "approved for IPP" items, I lost the majority of my clothing and hygiene products, along with all my electronic devices and commissary food items. This reassignment by IPP to Daggett County Jail cost me over $1,500 of accumulated, approved property. My choices were to give it away, pay to have it mailed out, or arrange for someone to pick it up within 30 days. I then spent the next 6 months replacing socks, underwear, t-shirts, thermals, shorts, etc. This added up to several thousands more dollars. It was absurd to me that I had to replace the very items I had been forced to get rid of; especially when they were allowed to be purchased in the next facility I was incarcerated in.

The housing section in Daggett County was another big letdown. It was a 14-man dorm built to house 12 inmates. That meant, being the new kid on the block, there wasn't a place to sit and eat my meals. I had to eat on the floor or sit on an ice chest until at least two people left and I moved up the ranks of seniority. I couldn't sit on my bed and eat because I had a top bunk and I wasn't going to eat food above someone else's bed. That's basic prison etiquette. So, I took my place eating on the floor.

In prison, everything is done by seniority. Daggett County was no exception. I would have to wait my turn to use the phone, watch TV, exercise in the mini yard, get employment, take a shower etc. I would remain the new "fish" until someone left and I took their spot. The only other way to move up the ranks is to fight and I wasn't about to do that. This incredibly small housing section only exacerbated the problems for new guys and I would just have to wait my turn.

The housing section was pie-shaped with 2-man bunks along the two outside walls. The shower, two toilets and two sinks were at the back with the entrance to the section at the

146

front. In the center of the room were two tables that sat six people each with a walkway between the bunks and tables. That walkway was less than 20 inches wide. It was a tiny space.

Movement out of the section was pretty limited. They offered LDS Institute, LDS Addiction Recovery and a couple of Programming classes at night. School was held Monday through Friday in the afternoons. These classes were held in the MPR (Multi-Purpose Room) which was about ten feet by fifteen feet at best. You could work out for an hour each day in the tiny gym that housed a handful of free weights and one universal machine. When the weather got warmer, you were able to go out into the main yard for 90 minutes about every two weeks. The main yard was a small chain-linked enclosure that had a half of a basketball court and two horseshoe stakes. It was possible to walk laps while other inmates took turns playing basketball but there wasn't enough room to actually run. On Sunday, you could attend church services in a small modular out-building on the other side of the main yard. Other than that, you were sequestered to the section and left to contend with the same inmates day in and day out. It felt very much like being on a 23-hour lockdown with a bigger cell and few extra amenities.

The section was so small that you couldn't work out or walk laps without causing all kinds of contention. Everyone was on top of each other and very much on edge all of the time. The Cost of Commissary was about double what it was at CUCF and phone calls were nearly triple the normal, astronomical cost. There were no employment opportunities for the first 12 months and they were only menial labor jobs; being a janitor or working in the kitchen. All visits were barrier only, meaning no physical contact with your visiting family members. Dinner every night was a sack lunch. Breakfast and lunch meals were generally hot and better than average. I never thought I would be missing "normal" prison life, but I was.

For the first two weeks I remained on my bunk trying to figure out what to do next. I was severely depressed and full of anxiety. I couldn't afford to call anyone and it was virtually impossible to use the section tables. Crap was strewn from one end of the tables to the other. I'm amazed that anyone had room to sit down and eat. There were empty bowls and cups and clutter all over the tables. The only thing that seemed acceptable to me was to lay on my bunk and keep my thoughts to myself. From there I could get a handle on everyone's personality.

If you had $90 you could purchase a portable DVD player and then negotiate taking your turn at watching the DVDs that came in and out of the sections. It was impossible to do anything really productive. When I first came to prison, I made a commitment to myself to make every day count. I had been determined to identify the flaws that had brought me to prison and change every one of them with a concerted, daily effort. Here, I was at a loss. What was the purpose of this? How would I make good on my commitment to make every day count? How was I going to live this way for at least another four years? It was horrific!

After two or three weeks I was called into the MPR by the county jail school teacher and given some answers to some of my questions. Prior to this, I had been corresponding with the founder of the PrisonEd Foundation and apparently he knew the teacher at the jail and referred my services to her. She called me in and wanted to know if I was interested in helping out her and the school? After my experience at CUCF with getting on the bad side of the Warden etc., I wanted no part of that but I really needed a job. She asked me to help out with the USU Herbarium Project. Having absolutely no idea what herbarium meant or what the project required, I agreed. To my recollection it was the first time I had even heard the word. At this point it didn't really matter. It would get me out of the section 2 hours every morning and that is what I needed if I was going to survive this place.

The USU Herbarium Project restored some of my purpose while housed at Daggett County. My job was to review digital photographs and catalog the information written in those photographs into the Herbarium Database used by USU and other colleges and universities. It was brainless work that only required typing skills and an attention to detail.

After a couple of weeks, I asked if I could join the afternoon class and work on my PrisonEd Foundation homework. PrisonEd Foundation distributes college level materials to inmates who want to increase their education beyond secondary levels. The founder and I met a few times at CUCF while the principal and I were developing UPrep academy. PrisonEd was integral to our beginnings and provided much of the curriculum for UPrep until we could get our own curriculum up and running and until we could engage Salt Lake Community College and Snow College in the process.

I was taking Beginning Spanish and Math 1010 and needed a place outside the section where I could concentrate. The teacher obliged me and I began working on my studies in her classroom every afternoon.

My time for personal study became fairly short lived as I got to know the teacher more and saw the need for what we had created at CUA inside CUCF. I determined to type up a proposal to bring CUA/Outreach to Daggett County Jail. It took several weeks to draft the 80+ page proposal that outlined the details of the program. The local high school principal perused the proposal and determined it was too much. The only concession he was willing to give was to allow the teacher to hire an inmate as a full-time tutor so direct instruction could be given to a handful of inmates. Though a start, it fell horribly short of the program we created at CUCF.

I was offered the tutor position but since the "program" to be implemented fell horribly short of what was possible, I declined. Instead, I returned to the section and started my own ad-hock instructional program. Along with another inmate who was well versed in self-improvement initiatives, we started taking turns teaching courses on everything from behavior modification to financial literacy. We used books like "How to Win Friends and Influence People" and "Think and Grow Rich" to help our students learn to better communicate and get along with other people. We taught subjects in which we had real life experience; budgeting and money management, real estate, business building and the stock market. We found several inmates with expertise in an area and invited them to build and teach a course. Every afternoon we would have 6-8 inmate/students sitting around the table learning anything we had to offer. They were intrigued and attentive. It was the same response we had found in CUCF when we started CUA/Outreach and UPrep. Unbeknownst to the UDC, most inmates want to learn and want to change.

We had a strong desire to go bigger so we went around the principal who had pretty much denied my previous education proposal and went straight to the superintendent of schools. One of the LDS volunteers was the county mayor and the wife of the superintendent. Several other LDS volunteers were involved in county government. Over the past year, we had been participating in their programs and we had the opportunity to get to know them. More importantly, they got to know us. We felt that these people could apply the necessary pressure on the jail commander and sheriff to allow us to begin what we were proposing as a Tiered Rehabilitation Program.

Everyone agreed to meet and discuss the proposal. It took four hours to lay out the groundwork and cover the details. By the time we were done, each person in attendance was in complete agreement. All we would have to do is bring the

Jail Commander and Sheriff on board. All they would need to do is say yes. The program we proposed, similar to the one established in CUA inside CUCF, would be completely self-funded and would require nothing from the facility or officers except cooperation. We would model our program after CUA and would access the same funding pools based on our outcomes and successes. Then we would move to becoming self-funding and completely self-sufficient through a vocational training program that produced products that could be sold to the public or government agencies. The program would be tiered so that inmates would progress through the self-realization, education and behavior modification parts of the program into a vocational training program. Upon completion, they would be in position to become positive, productive members of society with the personal, emotional, social and vocational skills to succeed. It was a no brainer.

Enter the perfect storm. Two weeks later, the entire Daggett County Jail was shut down by the UDC. Come to find out, two guards and a handful of inmates had mutually agreed and instigated several incidents of horseplay. Without going into detail, the two officers were charged with felony assault and the 80 state inmates were moved to other facilities.

The Draper Prison – A welcome relief from the County Jail

After 14 months in county jail, I was happy to be back at a prison. Once again, however, all my property was confiscated, which meant that I had to make arrangements to send it out. Apparently my socks, underwear, t-shirts, thermals, shorts and sweats weren't allowed at the Draper Facility. I couldn't keep my CD player, CD's, books, dictionary, calculator or several other items either. Interestingly, with the exception of the CD player, all of these items could be purchased on commissary at Draper. I

151

was out $300 or so in property. In spite of that and though the Draper Prison is no picnic, anything beats most county jails.

I spent my first two or three weeks in Draper in what seemed to be actual hell. It was like fishing in all over again, only this time I wasn't entering gladiator school. Within three days of arrival, two of the inmates that transferred with me from Daggett were jumped and robbed of all their belongings. They literally stole the clothes off their backs, the shoes off their feet, and what little personal property they had left. And then to drive the point home, they proceeded to stomp them out with their feet. The housing section was flooded with drugs which created a need to steal from more fortunate inmates so they could "sell" their stolen goods for another fix.

Illegal activity was everywhere. Inmates were constantly gangbanging, fighting, tattooing, stealing, batching hooch and getting high. I couldn't believe this could happen in a prison! I knew I had to figure a way out of there.

Within three weeks I was transferred to another housing unit. Though it was far less chaotic, I still had a couple inmates check my paperwork to see if I was a sex offender before I was "allowed" to move in to my cell. I ended up staying there for about four months. I had a decent Cellie and knew a handful of the guys in the section. Two of them had been my students while I was working at CUA years earlier. Since they were significant members in their respective gangs, I was considered off limits to everybody. That meant that I wouldn't be targeted or made to be somebody's victim. That being said, I still had to be on my toes and figure out how to navigate the social nightmare that is prison life.

To avoid getting caught up in the mix, I signed up for six Programming classes but Corrections wouldn't allow that. I could only take one. It wasn't like CUCF where Programming and productive time had come to be the norm.

Since I couldn't stay busy in Programming, I started applying for every job I could find, anything to get out of the section during the day. Luckily, I was accepted by the UCI furniture shop. I was also able to enroll in the "Stop Domestic Violence" treatment program.

In the beginning, the UCI job consumed most of my time. Thankfully, it was mandatory to work six days a week through the busy season that ran from sometime in March through July. Initially I started out making 60 cents an hour and spent the day making drawer boxes for desks and filing cabinets. After about 4 months, my pay increased to $1 an hour and I started working the CNC machines. Learning to work and program them was a welcome challenge. I was finding purpose in what I was doing so my time was getting easier.

Things were beginning to balance out. I moved over to the sex offender housing unit and was housed in a worker dorm. Typically, because I am a kappa, I wouldn't be allowed to be in sigmas but I got an override by my supervisor. The unit I was in only contained about 40% sex offenders. The remainder of us were omegas and kappas on overrides. Though Corrections wouldn't refer to it as a sex offender unit, the rest of the prison saw it that way. I really didn't care what it was called. It was comfortable and the sex offenders (SOs) pretty much stay to themselves and everybody else is too mild mannered to care about prison life politics. I was glad to be out of the other section. I no longer had to watch my back or wonder if I would come home one day and have all my property stolen.

I was pretty lucky that I got to stay in Draper. Within 90 days every one of the inmates who had been moved from Daggett County had been IPP'd back out to county. I thank my attorney for working with the IPP director to ensure I could stay in Draper and work on my special attention and not have to go back to a county jail.

Once I settled into my new housing assignment and completed the Domestic Violence treatment program, I signed up for Salt Lake Community College courses. SLCC had received a chunk of money from the State Legislature to provide post-secondary education to inmates. They were working closely with UPrep down in Gunnison and were also providing opportunities in Draper. The program was based on the funding described and the need for any participants to sign a promissory note that they would repay the costs of education once released. Each semester I enrolled with the hope that eventually I would earn my associate's degree. I knew that this could open several new doors for me once I received parole and returned to civilian life.

Even though the furniture shop and SLCC consumed most of my time, I felt like my life was more in balance than it had been since I was taken from CUCF. I had regular contact visits and phone calls with my family. I was making enough money that I was building up my savings again. I was eating healthier and able to exercise a couple of nights a week. On the weekends, I could run laps around the main yard. I went to LDS church services every Sunday and attended addiction recovery classes. I was reading more and watching less TV. During that time, I lost 20 or 30 pounds. Most importantly, we had finished my Special Attention and were ready to submit it to the Board of Pardons.

As I mentioned earlier, the BOPP agreed to move up my rehearing from June 2020 to November 2018. I would still have to wait another six months to be seen by them but I was ready. Since I was already over my matrix, and considering all the programs, work, etc. that I had done since being incarcerated, I had hopes for an immediate release. During that six months I was determined to stay the course. I had found my pace.

Unfortunately, that didn't last. Because of a grievance with visiting, I was again rolled up, this time back to CUCF.

Back to CUCF

In the move to CUCF, I lost another $300 in personal property. That may not sound like much but at $.40 to $1.00 per hour, it is. It is hard to understand why, when transferring from one prison to another, an inmate would not be allowed to keep his books and headphones, etc. It makes no sense. I asked my first wife to contact the UDC director and report that the transfer was a retaliatory measure. She received word back that in fact it wasn't and was just part of standard procedure to accommodate the needs of the two facilities. She asked if this was going to be a permanent transfer or if I would be IPP'd out to county. He assured her that I would remain in Gunnison until my hearing in 13 weeks.

If the move wasn't a form of retaliation, it is ironic that I ended up on the roughest housing unit in CUCF. I immediately applied to go to STRIVE but was denied by the Gale Captain. According to the three staff members who were trying to help me, the captain saw me as entitled and wasn't going to accommodate me. It was clear to me that the blackballing that had started three years ago in CUCF was being continued.

Not to be deterred, I looked around and saw a unit full of people that needed help with their education. I quickly settled in and "set up shop." Most of the inmates knew who I was and started coming to me for help with their studies. It was a win/win. This allowed me to focus in on some BOPP items. I began exercising every day and running laps in the afternoon. I attended a couple of classes in Education to brush up on my algebra and computer skills. I would take some time each week to sit down with the principal to talk about CUA and the great progress and success it was having. I limited that time, however, to avoid anyone getting the idea that I wanted back in the CUA workforce.

155

Visiting was much better. Though she had to drive south to Gunnison, my first wife could visit without harassment or feeling uncomfortable.

It was satisfying to see the CUA/Outreach and UPrep programs that I had been so closely involved with were not just thriving but growing. The school boasted over 1,000 students enrolled in CUA/Outreach and had peaked at 280 UPrep students. Unfortunately, because of the culture problem that exists, the principal was in a constant battle with the powers that be to keep it going. UPrep had been cut dramatically from 280 students to about 80, for example, for "security" reasons. They had decided that having more than 30 inmates at a time in the education corridor with only one officer was a security risk. I had to roll my eyes when I heard that. Both Programming and Education hosted over 150 inmates at night and on the weekends for over 5 years with zero problems. Now, Programming was allowed to continue the practice but education was limited to 30 inmates.

None of this was a surprise. Even though CUA/Outreach and UPrep had grown, it was a constant fight with the leadership of CUCF. Many of the housing unit officers understood our value. However, the mindset that we were inmates and didn't deserve anything is overpowering. Allowing inmates to better themselves and prepare to return to society wasn't gonna happen on their watch. It doesn't matter that all the data backs up the fact that changing behavior takes time, effort and education. The only way to reduce recidivism is to educate emotionally, socially, intellectually and occupationally.

The UDC has many problems but the biggest is the culture of "us vs them." It may be the case that as inmates, we don't deserve anything. However, society – the taxpayers – deserve a rehabilitated person at parole, not someone that has learned all the wrong things. Until that one thing changes, little hope is on the horizon.

The saddest part of all this for me is that the principal, the author of this book, retired at the end of that school year. Without question the inmates at CUCF lost their greatest advocate. And, if the UDC ever chose to be honest about it, they would have to admit that they lost their greatest advocate as well. That was the beauty of this man. He had a way of bringing the opposing sides together. I watched him do it over and over again. I imagine that in the end, he just got tired of having his spirit crushed by the powers that be. I imagine he lost hope.

The teacher who replaced me to run CUA/Outreach left at the same time. I'm told that within months of Mark's retirement, both CUA/Outreach and UPrep are in the process of being downsized. It appears that Education at CUCF is being returned to its "business as usual" UDC approach. Corrections seems to be working to erase it all.

Weber County Jail: Hell on Earth

I was only in Gunnison 8 weeks this time. So much for the staying there the 13 weeks until my rehearing promise. I was once again IPP'd out to county jail. This time to Weber County. Weber is one of the worst county jails in the state. By now my rehearing was five weeks out and scheduled to be held at CUCF. They had transferred me three hours south to Gunnison so they could turn around 8 weeks later and transfer me 4 hours north to Weber County only to make me return to CUCF 5 weeks later for the rehearing. What part of that makes any sense?

Once again I had to relinquish all my personal property and have it sent out. This time I was out about $600. Ironically, I had just purchased a TV that had not arrived. The $185 TV arrived after I was taken to Weber County. Even though I was no longer there, my name was engraved on it and it was "mine." About three weeks after my transfer I received a letter from UDC property saying that I needed *to pay $19.75 to have a TV that I had never actually received, sent out. They cited that even though I hadn't signed for it or actually received it; it was still mine because it had been engraved. I was speechless. My first wife traveled to Gunnison and retrieved it with the rest of my personal property and took it to Salt Lake and placed it with an entire closet full of my confiscated property from prison. When I am finally released I will have enough underwear to last two or three years and a 13" TV that Deseret Industries won't even accept as a contribution. Mix that with all the dictionaries, books, calculators, watches, CD players, DVD players, hot pots, headphones and everything else and you have a quite a compilation of items that could not be transferred from one facility to another even though most of the "old" items were allowed in the next facility.*

The transfer to Weber was particularly difficult. Come to find out that no toothpaste or soap or deodorant or lotion that had been opened was allowed into the facility. I wasn't allowed to have my MP3 player, writing materials, or any of my clothing items. They did allow me to keep my eye glasses but not the case I put them in. It was absurd!

Everything in the facility was cost prohibitive. Commissary was three to four times more expensive than it had been at CUCF. Phone calls were nearly double the cost and 10 minutes shorter. 15-minute video visits were allowed twice a week and were free provided your visitor would travel to the facility. There were no barrier or contact visits. Letter writing was not allowed either. To correspond, you had to either use a 3x5 postcard or pay two cents a minute to use their message service, kind of like text messaging.

The section was made up of four 12-man dorms with a day room only large enough to enclose its tables. We were allowed out of our dorms and into the day room 3 times a day; 4 hours in the morning, 3 hours in the afternoon and an hour and a half in the evening. Other than that we were confined to our dorm which had barely enough room for the toilet and sink and not enough room to exercise and move around.

Movement wasn't allowed outside the housing unit. Even church was held in a small room on the unit. Every couple of days for 30 minutes we were allowed "yard" time in the enclosed concrete box outside the section. This allowed for little else but handball. There wasn't a main yard or any access to see outside. There was little to no natural light and no Education or Programming. It was literally a warehouse for inmates.

The food was absolutely horrendous. Everyday breakfast consisted of cornflakes, a milk type product (not real milk) and biscuits with either a slice of bologna or a scoop of peanut butter mixed with grape jelly. Lunch and dinner weren't much better. They consisted of watered down gravy with either rice, potatoes or noodles. That came with a side of vegetables, a green salad, roll and 8 ounces of "fortified juice." On occasion, as a treat, the gravy had small pieces of processed meat. For dessert we were given canned fruit. The meals were high calorie and low nutrition.

Weber County Jail has to be one of the most chaotic facilities in the state. They housed county, state and federal inmates all together, creating all kinds of political bias and racial contention. County inmates are awaiting case resolution or serving out less than a one-year term. These inmates are usually detoxifying and unpredictable. Most are in the midst of losing everything that is important to them while watching their life diminish day by day. State inmates have already gone through that experience, done time in either Draper or CUCF and are now back "in the box." They have lost all their personal property. Any previous prison life with any possibility of hope is now gone. They have either done most of their time and are getting close to the gate or they still have a lot of time to do but are not an escape threat and the last place they want to be is warehoused in a county jail constantly turning over with local inmates. Federal inmates are also waiting case resolution but unlike county inmates, they are faced with the reality of long mandatory sentences. This constant state of flux takes its toll on everybody and keeps them all on edge. Then add prison and gang politics and you have a recipe for disaster. I have experienced my share of prison and gang politics. This was a whole new level. It was madness!

Despite all that was going on around me, I did my best to stay productive and keep to myself. Initially I worked on writing out my 30-day transition plan. I wanted to prepare a copy for the BOPP and give it to them at my hearing. I would write it all out and then transcribe it over the tablet to my first wife who would forward it to my attorney for review. I had it in my head that the BOPP would expect a detailed outline of my intentions upon release concerning my housing and employment, treatment etc. When I wasn't working on that project, I was helping other inmates work on their pre-sentencing packets or write their accountability letters for their judge.

To Draper then CUCF then Back Again

About a week before seeing the BOPP I was transferred back to Draper, then to CUCF for the hearing, then back to Draper before being returned to Weber County Jail. I gave up asking why a long time ago. By the time I met with the BOPP I was sleep deprived, exhausted, unshaven and disoriented. During those 10 days I was housed in level 2. That means 23-hour lockdown without access to visits, my attorney or writing materials. Each day I had a different Cellie. My clothes were unlaundered and I wasn't given any deodorant, Chapstick or lotion. The only items I was allowed was a legal board packet. Everything else was left at the property room at Weber County Jail. UDC did provide me with a 2" toothbrush, generic toothpaste, a bar of soap, like you get in a motel, and a comb. That was it for the 10 days.

My BOPP hearing did not go well. My two oldest daughters made extremely emotional pleas for my release but that went unheard. I was repeatedly interrupted in the middle of my sentences and was playing catchup throughout the entire hearing. I felt like everything I said was in one way or another used against me. My accountability, remorse and apologies were diminished and dismissed by the hearing officer. Nothing I had accomplished; the classes, the self-help, the Education, the employment, the service was discussed. The transition plan was barely brought up. By the end of the hearing I was speechless and feeling lower than the day I committed my crimes. The entire scenario was surreal. It was like a dream, a nightmare.

When I got back to Weber County, they tried putting me into a different housing section. I told them that wasn't going to work for me. It takes a great deal of effort and maneuvering to get your bearings in a new section and I wasn't in the mood to start over. I made it clear that they could send me back to the section I originally fished into, they could place me in solitary confinement or have the prison come pick me up and take me back to Draper. After about four hours they relented and sent me back "home," back to my section. It is amazing what a person can actually be grateful for.

I went the following week without any of my personal property. I kept making requests on the tablet communication system they used and they kept saying that they had already returned it to me. Try as I may, they wouldn't listen. I was at the end of my rope. With almost no exceptions, to that point, I had done all I could while in prison to be respectful to the officers. In spite of their continual contempt, I had done my best to maintain my composure and be respectful of my captors. I felt it was the right thing to do. With this I finally snapped. I was at the end of my rope. One afternoon as one of the property officers was delivering the property to a new fish in my section, I unkindly told her that I had not received my property, that it had been 10 days and that the lack of concern was ridiculous. I included a few other choice words that I'm not proud of. It wasn't my proudest moment but I was sick and tired of being unheard. It had been a very difficult, emotional, discouraging week. Later that night, at about 1 am, they brought me all my stuff. Apparently it was sitting in the property room, under a desk in an unmarked bag. I apologized for losing my cool. They did not apologize for misplacing my property.

The next couple of weeks I spent contemplating my future. I knew the hearing hadn't gone well. Even so, I was sure they were going to let me go. After all, there was nothing left to take from me. I had completed every program I could get into, I had helped countless others improve their education, I was a model inmate. I was significantly over sentencing matrix. It was my turn to go home.

Then I started having doubts. I contacted everyone who had come to the hearing. Like me, they thought the hearing officer had been tough. They felt that I had handled myself well and had responded well to his questions. Like me, they thought that it was my time. Everyone's hopes were high.

My release date was posted online and everyone, including myself was left wondering. Two and a half more years. Their decision made no sense. It was unfair, inhumane, and devastating.

Within minutes of hearing the decision over the phone I began to plot my course for earning time credits. The Utah Legislators had approved house bill 348 several years previously that outlines the conditions for earning and receiving time credits. Now that the BOPP had given me a date, I just needed to complete my current mapping and participate in a JRI approved vocational training program. If I aligned things perfectly, then I could earn 8-12 months off my remaining sentence. That would leave about 18 months.

I immediately set about a plan that would get me into an approved program. It was not easy. The caseworker who helped me develop my plan and then submit it. He was ... noncommittal. He made excuses and showed little real interest. Since I was confident that the UDC would not allow me to participate in another substance abuse treatment program, (that would by my third) I determined to follow a vocational option. The caseworker was sure that IPP would never allow me to leave Weber and that I would serve out my time there. Nonetheless, I determined to find my way back to Draper and participate in the DATC program. While at Draper, I figured that I could participate in several programs simultaneously. I could finish up the UCI apprenticeship program and take some more community college classes towards my associates degree. That would easily equate to 12 months of time credits. However, to get there I had two major obstacles; IPP and my caseworker.

I made several attempts over the next two weeks to again see my caseworker. He didn't respond so I had my first wife contact the IPP director who then contacted the IPP deputy warden who then had my caseworker contact me. It worked. We met for several hours and discussed the possible scenarios. He remained difficult and noncommittal. Finally after weeks of pleading, he agreed that if I would write the required amends letters to the members of my family and get him the list of recreational activities I plan to explore upon release he would request a 4-month time cut to the BOPP.

Purgatory, A Welcome Relief

Two weeks after completing the above, I found myself on my way the Purgatory, the Washington County Jail. Apparently, Weber County had lost their contract with the UDC.

Today I am housed at the newly built community Corrections center of Washington County. This is an outbuilding of the PCF (Purgatory Correctional Facility) that contains two dorm sections that can house up to 56 inmates each. I live in a worker dorm and currently there are only 22 of us here. The space is a welcome relief. Everyone in the dorm is a level 4 state inmate. That means that they are well behaved and have a good prison record and have less than three years. We all qualify for a "gate pass" which means we can work outside the fences. In a nutshell, we provide labor to the local government agencies to do routine maintenance.

As far as incarceration facilities go, this one is pretty good. Commissary is fairly inexpensive; the food is the best I've ever had since serving time and we can have 60 minutes a week of free video visits. Contact visits are allowed twice a week in the lobby for up to two hours. There is an outdoor mini-yard that is open two hours a day. It isn't huge but it is outdoors and provides ample room to exercise. The section shares a flat screen TV on which we can watch movies and play video games.

On the flipside, there is still a bit of a county jail mentality. Phone calls are expensive and most all written communication must take place on a tablet at a cost of 5 cents a minute. The only mail is on an ax or ax post card in or out. Shoe laces are not allowed and neither is most of your personal property. We are allowed MP3 players in our dorm but not in the rest of the facility. In the worker dorm there is no access to Education or Programming or even church services. Our only privilege outside the section is to work.

We work about 8 hours a day on various work crews. We average about 170 hours a month and get paid $.85 an hour. That equates to about $140 a month. Sadly, I spend more than that a month to stay connected with my family.

Our days are spent mowing lawns, pulling weeds and picking up garbage. We do the landscaping for all the county buildings and when we don't have anything else to do, we pick up trash along I-15 or along one of the many state roads in the area. The work is mostly mindless and can be very monotonous but is necessary. Mostly I'm good with it but then sometimes I feel like I'm spinning my wheels and not really accomplishing anything. One of my regrets before incarceration was that I spent too much time focusing on my work and not enough time focusing on my family.

Ironically, I feel like I'm in a situation where I'm being forced to go back to the life I lived before coming to prison. My incarceration has brought me to the point of serving and helping others on a personal level. Not a day goes by that I don't think of ways to help my family and friends improve themselves and become better. I do the same for myself. In a weird way, I feel like I'm being forced to regress from my reformed state and live like I lived prior to coming to prison. I do my best to refute this notion and accept the things that I cannot change by taking one day at a time. I truly believe there is purpose in this current experience for me and that I'm not just wasting time. In spite of that, I still feel pretty useless and unchallenged.

Every day I wonder if I can serve my last 18 months out here. However, the time has flown by and that gives me hope. Nonetheless, at the end of the day, when I do my personal inventory, I know that I have failed at making this day count. It's as if my whole purpose has been sucked up and placed 18 months down the road.

If the Corrections system were really about rehabilitation and could readily evaluate individuals who had truly changed, Edmond would have been released years ago, once his debt to society was paid. One might argue that he hasn't paid his debt. However, no one showed up to either of his hearings to argue against his release. His victim has moved out of state. He is many years over his minimum sentence. His response from the board is in fact that in their opinion he is not rehabilitated. Their claim is that it will take another 18 months. During those 18 months, there will be no therapy nor will there be any education. He will be doing menial labor. Not much rehab in that process.

It's all pretty random and arbitrary. From his case, it is clear that the current system is not about rehabilitation, it is about punishment. Furthermore, it is not capable of making any kind of concerted effort towards rehabilitation. Any time rehabilitation takes place, it is completely in the hands of the individual who must constantly fight the system in order to succeed. In the current system accurate assessment is impossible. Again, I don't think that by and large the people who make up the UDC or the BOPP are bad people. I see the antiquated, inept system as the culprit. Oh, and a misused IPP system. Something that could be changed if only someone in authority had a vision.

Chapter 20

Good Cop/Bad Cop—
Good Inmate/Bad Inmate

"There is good and Bad in Everyone"
Stevie Wonder and Paul McCartney

I have said this before and I'd like to say it again, being sent to prison has been one of the most fulfilling, eye opening and enjoyable professional experiences of my life. It has, without a doubt, helped me understand people at a level I never thought possible. The idea that I would have this experience in my life is surreal.

One of the most impactful parts of the experience has to do with the people I've met. Had I stayed in the public education world, I would never have met and become friends with literally hundreds of people that currently bless my life.

When I first fished in, I was amazed at how many people knew me or at least knew who I was. Being a high school basketball coach in rural Utah for 23 years comes with a good deal of notoriety. I would go to different housing units and be quickly recognized by many of the guards.

As the principal of CUA, I found myself going to each of the housing units to visit with different Corrections personnel about different issues. Sometimes it was during weekly OMR and other times I would take a more personal approach having conversations in an office or corridor. In the early days I was a bit nervous. I would try to be careful to always keep in the company of the guys in blue. However, as time went on, I felt completely safe with the guys in white. It was unexpected.

To illustrate, let me relate an experience. I had been at CUA about three months when, at the end of one such visit in the Elm Housing Unit, I was walking out the corridor that leads from the unit to the central corridor. At this point four housing unit hallways come together like spokes on a wheel leading to a hub. The slider in front of me started to close. Without knowing why the door had shut, I pushed the intercom button and the officer in the bubble gave me the explanation. Come to find out, the officers were doing a controlled move. That's a situation where the cops were moving a level 2 inmate, (an inmate on 23 hours lockdown) in shackles from one location to another. Procedure is that when that happens, no one but the officers can be in the same room, corridor, or area as the shackled inmate. I was a little nervous but since I was alone in the hallway, it wasn't a big deal.

Less than a minute later a group of inmates started making their way from their cells towards the bubble and the closed slider where I was waiting. Within a short time, 15 inmates stood by me in the corridor waiting for the door to open. I don't know if my newfound companions knew it or not, but I was extremely nervous. I started looking for options but found none. I could either wait it out or start running and screaming back through the gauntlet of inmates that had formed between myself and the only escape that I could see. After what seemed like five minutes, while I was contemplating my options, the slider opened and we all walked through the door to the common corridor around the bubble. I very nonchalantly walked towards several officers and made conversation. I can't tell you the relief I felt. I've always thought I was a pretty tough guy but ... not that day.

About 14 months later I found myself in the exact same situation. As I headed down the hallway from the Fir Captain's office, the slider closed in front of me. Movement started and the hallway soon filled up with inmates. This time, however, was much different. I recognized many of them and they knew me as well. Several said hello and a couple others addressed me by name and started asking questions about Education and this or that situation they needed help with. When the slider opened, I walked with that group of 15 or so inmates into the bubble corridor, out the hallway that led to the quarter-mile walkway connecting the Boulders with the Henries, and on into the Education/Programming corridor. We talked the entire time. I was sitting in my office before I realized what had just happened. I had spent at least 10 minutes pretty much alone with a dozen or more inmates and felt perfectly safe, perfectly comfortable.

Of all the valuable realizations of my experience inside CUCF is that there are good people, lots of them, who wear white jumpsuits (yes white, not orange or striped). I don't want to marginalize the fact that these men have done terrible things to get where they are and have likewise victimized and hurt other people. They have, and that debt needs to be paid. I addressed that in the introduction and encourage you to take a look at the introduction again if you are getting the feeling I am in any way minimizing that fact. But I have found that many of these men recognize and accept that they have hurt people terribly and truly regret it. They don't like it and don't want to repeat it. Like any of us they can't change the past. The inmates who want to change must leave that behind, though it haunts them every day, and look to the present with hope for a better future. The inmates/people that work towards doing that are the ones that evolve, change and become better people.

Fast-forward eight years; because of requests from security, I do my best to not get caught alone in any area with inmates. It's a good policy and I agree with it. However, no matter where I go in this facility, inmates greet me warmly. Most know me by name and most appreciate Education and what we do to provide them opportunity to change. Thus, "All My Friends are Felons."

Education works very closely with the security staff. Inside our corridor there are twelve classrooms, three administration offices, a security desk and three or four security officers. We all feel very safe. In fact, I believe we are safer here inside the prison than most teachers are out in the public school world. Not only because of the security officers present but also because of the great respect the large majority of inmates hold for our Education staff. In the Education corridor, we do all we can to treat the students with value and respect. That, in and of itself, creates a safe place for us to work.

That being said, there are still a number of inmates who cannot be trusted and are still looking for ways to victimize anyone and everyone. Prisons are full of predators, gang bangers and drugs; all the things that one might expect.

To illustrate that point I would like to relate one of the most difficult and troubling experiences of my time "down."

It had to do with a faculty member that was gaslighted by an inmate. When I fished in, the previous director gave me a book entitled, "The Games Inmates Play." It was a book full of actual stories of how inmates had gamed staff and officers. It was a bit of a doomsday look at inmates but I found it valuable and made it required reading for all new staff members.

In July of 2014 we hired a new faculty member. She was a really good teacher. She related well with people and had a solid ability to engage students in learning. Like all new staff members, I gave her a copy of "the Games Inmates Play."

One of the key aspects of working in a prison is to not get isolated. As a faculty and staff, we worked together to stay solidified as a group. We often ate lunch together. The faculty shared a common office and there was great camaraderie. Jane fit in very well and made good friendships with several of the other female faculty members.

However, over a short period of time, Jane began to withdraw from her peers. No one knew why but she became more and more isolated. She often skipped going to lunch with her group. She spent more and more time in her classroom and less time in the faculty administration office and her mood and temperament changed. Since she was new, her friends concluded that it was her personality and that it would pass.

Skipping to the end of the story, I got a phone call from internal investigations. Jane had been drawn in by her inmate tutor. Over about 6 weeks, this inmate had convinced her that he ran the prison. She was convinced that this inmate told the warden what to do, that he had complete control of the place. This sounds impossible, but if you read any quality information on gaslighting, you can begin to understand how it could happen. It wasn't anything to do with the teacher, except that she didn't take into account the stories she had read in "The Games Inmates Play."

Though she had done nothing illegal, the potential was very high that she could. It was a very dangerous situation. Within days, she was "escorted off property," the inmate was sent to Hickory, a 23 hour lockdown housing unit, and our staff had a briefing on what had happened and how to prevent it. It was a very hard learning experience for all of us, especially for Jane.

The inmate involved was a textbook gaslighter. It was scary how he had got in her head and convinced her of an imaginary reality. It was a classic example of the games inmates play.

The problem is, because of these scenarios, it is not uncommon for officers to treat all inmates the same, failing to recognize that all people are different and all inmates are different. Many officers view them only as felons. As felons, they are all the same and don't deserve anything. I believe that is a result of the culture that is nurtured by the Corrections system. In my orientation, I was told that all

171

inmates are the same and need to be treated the same. As I have worked within Corrections, I found that regular officers are similarly treated all the same. Education is treated all the same. It is like the army. All recruits are treated the same. In the army, that creates a viable and responsive group that can save each other's lives. There it may have value. I suppose it works for them. It does little to develop people on an individual basis and it won't work in a prison system.

People are people. We are all human beings. We come in all shapes and sizes from all different kinds of backgrounds. As Paul McCartney and Stevie Wonder said in his song *Ebony and Ivory,* "There is good and bad in everyone." Inmates have good and bad. Police have good and bad. There is good and bad in all walks of life.

I worked very closely with a portion of the security staff at CUCF. Besides the four or five officers stationed in Education, I was consistently interacting with the security in each of the eight housing units, the security staff in Programming, the security staff in Corridor, and the administrative security staff of CUCF. They are by and large good people. Many are my neighbors. Many attend the same church. Others live in a neighboring town. Still others live in small towns some miles away. I would dare say that 70-80% of them come from a very similar background as myself. We share a rural culture that goes back generations and has a strong history of creating good people. Most of the officers I have worked with want to do the best they can at their jobs and want to do the right thing. I made good friends with many of the security staff at CUCF and appreciated their service and support.

In spite of that fact, there are some who "don't get that they don't get it." I wouldn't classify them as criminals or even exhibiting criminal behavior. It is just they don't see potential in any inmate.

A classic example is an officer that worked for more than five years in Education. Officer Johnson was from a small town in Central Utah. He was nice enough and was sure he had the perfect balance of good cop/good educator. He was a likeable guy. Problem was, he had all the right answers to all the wrong questions.

I can't speak to his motivation, though I could guess. On the surface he was always promoting Education. He would promote hope for change and the value of providing real opportunities for the 1,000 or so inmates we worked with every day. But then he would undermine our best efforts to help. I don't think for a minute he saw his activities as undermining. In fact, I'm sure he sees himself as the most pro-Education officer in the facility (he said so himself many times). But, he was a constant burr. He constantly found problems where there were none. On more than one occasion he requested one of our key inmate tutors be sent to another facility because in his opinion, the inmate was getting too familiar, entitled or empowered. He would report non-existent problems to his captain, creating a need for me to explain something that was superficial at best and non-existent at worse. He would on one side say good and yes and then on the other side say bad and no. He was able, through his tactics, to eliminate a good portion of our UPrep program simply by false reporting under the guise of support. It was not uncommon for inmates to report to me that Johnson had told them privately that in his opinion, they should serve their full sentence, no parole, and they should be locked up 23 hours a day.

What Johnson did wasn't illegal. It goes on in any organization. It is rare not to find a busy body who can't get onboard in any situation. And like all of us at one time or another, "they don't get that they don't get it." Johnson and others like him see all inmates as being the exact same. He couldn't see past their white jumpsuits or their past mistakes. He couldn't come to grips with the fact that they are all different and that they are all at different levels of progress. It is a foolish and unproductive way to live. Some inmates

173

are ready to be empowered and trusted while others cannot be trusted. And, of course, there are those in between. Making a distinction can be risky but, nothing ventured nothing gained.

Beyond that, there is the Gestapo type officer who seems to get a thrill from intimidation and domination. It is interesting who they are. Everybody knows them, both inmate and officer. Some are men. Some are women. They spend their time nitpicking. They love to find inmates or anyone for that matter making the slightest mistake. Their language is often poor and they treat the inmates like animals. They are constantly "poking the bear." Thankfully these types of officers are in the minority.

Much of Johnson' perception comes from the culture within the UDC that all inmates are the same, should be treated the same and all act the same. They are all predators. They are all looking for a way to victimize someone. They are low-life scums who can't be trusted. They will never change. It is unhealthy to think in such a way and it is very unproductive.

I could give many examples of good cops who had a much healthier attitude. One such example concerns an officer that I would end up hiring to be a teacher and then the Outreach Director of CUA. Michelle had spent about two years in Programming. She was security, not an instructor. From time to time, I would get input, good and bad from inmates on the security staff. She was always looking at the security side. She was careful and attentive, always on guard. At the same time, she had the ability to recognize good qualities and differentiate between the progressing inmate and the troublesome one. About a year before my retirement, we had a teacher leave and go to the public schools. One of the inmates on our inmate council suggested I hire her. We didn't know much about her. I didn't even know if she had a degree. I think that inmate visited with her and suggested she apply. The short story is, we hired her and within a year, she became our Outreach director.

This, by the way, underlines another characteristic of the UDC everyone should be treated the same.

In the case of Michelle, rather than sitting in the corridor monitoring inmates, her skills as an educator could have been put to use instructing class and directing other staffers and inmates in teaching. That is exactly what she is doing now at CUA and she is excellent at it.

I could make a list of all the other officers who like her treated the inmates with support and respect. Changing the culture of CUCF from a prison to a Correctional institution would not be that hard. There already exists a critical mass of officers who, if given the right culture, would jump on board.

The above is my perception concerning the matter. I would like to include the following excerpts from an article written by Brian Wood, a former inmate who writes for the *Ogden Standard-Examiner*, a newspaper in Ogden, Utah. He does a great job of describing the "us vs them" mentality that is the cause of great challenges in effecting the lasting change inmates need, the lasting change described in the UDC's own mission statement. (Refer to Chapter 1)

I know it's not politically correct, but I have an unpopular opinion about something, and I am going to share despite all the people who will probably get offended....

There's a stereotype that exists [among inmates] that officers are all a bunch of angry people who were picked on in high school. They are looked at that way even more so in Corrections. I don't know the cause, but there is [often] a bully mentality among officers. [From my perspective] the type of person who is drawn to the work in Corrections is often the exact opposite of the type of person who would be most effective in helping the prison population.

This is the point I never hear brought up when discussing programs and ideas on how to fix Corrections. The culture [often] exists among the staff that would have to buy-in and carry out any changes is not conducive to correction, growth and learning. There are all sorts of good-intentioned individuals in politics and society who have great ideas about how to fix Corrections, but before the culture is addressed, the best ideas will continue to be wasted. Too many officers believe their job is to punish inmates.

I heard the Captain of Programming at the time say, "If it were up to me, every one of you guys would be locked down for 23 hours per day for the duration of your sentence." This is the problem. If you believe that the job of Corrections is to punish, then you are part of the problem. Many officers were open about their disdain for prisoners.

I'm not suggesting we take justice out of the equation. I played scrabble with a convicted child molester, but that doesn't mean I want to see him released from prison; however, there is nothing positive that comes from hating other people.

I know some police officers that are great people; I also know some prisoners that are great people. There was one Corrections officer in particular who saw the good things I was doing in prison and contacted my family, encouraging them to visit. This man's whole reason for being a Corrections officer was to make a positive difference. He believed in the idea of correction and because of this, he was always at odds with his co-workers and the system. He would be the first to tell you that his career has been a battle. He created a program that had a ton of promise, but as it gained traction and really started to help inmates, it drew more opposition and was utterly sabotaged.

I was very proud to be part of the solution and found great fulfillment in the work I did in the prison with the CUA and the UPrep program. I don't have any data to back up my claims, but I said it before and I'll say it again, that

Educational program was the best thing the prison had going for it in the way of correction and helping the prison population. Sadly, the UPrep program that I and many others dedicated years of full-time work to is all but dismantled. The principal down in Gunnison and the volunteers and workers under him are still fighting the good fight, but my point is, there shouldn't be a fight.

The "us vs them" culture in the system is probably the biggest obstacle. There are guys on both sides who blindly hate the other group. That same officer who continues to fight and try to make a difference explained to me that while I am the enemy to many of his fellow officers, he was considered a traitor. Because of his efforts to help inmates and his desire to see them succeed, he was even more hated. Well, he was a hero to me and many others — he and the principal.

Here is another inmate experience, this one from Edmond as he was incarcerated in the Draper Prison. It relates to visiting and the challenges he and his visitor faced there.

I had again landed in the Draper Prison. As I mentioned earlier, the Board of Pardons (BOPP) agreed to move up my rehearing from June 2020 to November 2018. I would still have to wait another six months to be seen by them but I was ready. Since I was already over my matrix, and considering all the programs, work, etc. that I had done since being incarcerated, I had hopes for an immediate release. During that six months I was determined to stay the course. I had found my pace.

Unfortunately that didn't last. During this time, as my first wife would come in to visit me, she was being sexually harassed by one of the guards. This went on for several months unbeknownst to me. As she would come in, he would make constant inappropriate comments about the way she was dressed. He would make comments about how her shirt fit over her breasts and said that maybe he wouldn't let her visit me. Without telling me, she had made a couple of complaints via email but they went unanswered. I found out one day as she and I were visiting at the table in the visiting room. The sergeant walked up and made a comment about her being a vixen and then just walked away. I was completely stupefied. I couldn't believe he would say something like that to my female visitor. I was sure I had heard incorrectly but she assured me that this wasn't the first time.

At first, she didn't want to tell me about what was going on. Once she was convinced that I wouldn't overreact, she shared with me the details of the past several months. I was livid! But, as I had promised, I did not overreact. I asked her what she wanted to do about it and she expressed that she simply wanted it to stop.

We spent the rest of the visit discussing how we should move forward. I was in complete support of her reporting it to the powers that be. She was concerned that if she did that, they would retaliate against me. Though I felt she was right in that regard, we knew we had to do the right thing and stop this from happening to her or anyone else. As it turns out, there were others but like her, they likewise chose not to "rock the boat." Like us, they were afraid of retaliation. In the end, she reported it to the UDC director, and the warden with an email copy going to the governor's office and a local media source. This time her emails didn't go unnoticed. Within 20 minutes she was contacted and asked to have a sit-down with the warden and the UDC director.

The meeting took place a couple of weeks later with all three parties and my attorney. During this meeting, she was made to feel like it was all just a big misunderstanding and that she hadn't read the situation correctly. From her perspective, the meeting felt more like an interrogation of wrong-doing rather than an interview to find out the facts. She left the meeting feeling anxious and unheard. It was like she had done something wrong.

About three weeks later I was interviewed by the UDC internal investigations department. That's when the subtle acts of retaliation began taking place. During our visits, things changed. We were harassed for "hugging" too long. We could no longer sit side by side at the table. I sat on one side, she sat on the other. Several times, she was turned away because her shirt was the wrong color. They were shirts she had worn on prior visits but now they were not allowed, because of the color. Then the shakedowns began. Visiting would call over to my housing unit and have them shake me down on the way back to my unit after my visit. I had a metal watch, which I had a property contract for and had in my possession nearly the entire time I was in Draper. Suddenly I could no longer wear it outside my housing unit. I told them I was going to file a grievance. Within a couple weeks, I was sent to CUCF.

As far as we know, that visiting sergeant was never reprimanded for his inappropriate behavior. He kept his position in visiting the entire time the "investigation" was being conducted. Thankfully, he never made comments to me or my first wife. Nonetheless, she was very uncomfortable every time she saw him. He was unscathed while my life was once again turned upside down.

The bad cop problems that exist seem to come from three main sources. First, personality challenges among a small number of the staff. Those challenges exists in any group of people. They simply have to be identified and dealt with. The second source is the punitive culture problem that exists in the UDOC. We have addressed that multiple times in this book. The culture of the UDOC needs serious work and modification. The last source is boredom of the officers. We have also addressed this but to accentuate the fact I'd like to relate one additional experience.

In the summer of 2018 the sewer system in the Elm housing unit needed serious work. As a result of the construction, a portion of the walkway from the Boulders, where the Elm housing unit is located, to the Henries, where the main Education and Programming Corridors as well as Medical and Visiting are located, had to be closed and the inmates were re-routed through a maintenance access road still within the outer fences of the facility. The situation lasted for several months.

Since the new walk route was outside the normal path, security determined that officers needed to be posted to "direct traffic." As a result, two officers in a golf cart were posted at an intersection along the access road.

Most of the time inmates go from one activity/area to another during "movement" which generally occurs hourly at about 10 to the hour. However, there are other times when inmates have to move. For example, they may have to go to medical or to visiting.

One day, I heard inmates talking about an inmate they referred to as a "crash test dummy." I was curious about the conversation and was told this story:

While coming down to visit his parents, the inmate in question was walking along the detour described above. He walked past the two officers in the golf cart and as he got 20 or so yards away, the driver ran the cart towards him at full speed. He then slammed on the brakes with the intent of stopping just short of the inmate. Well, their judgement was poor. (In more ways than one). As a result, they literally ran over the inmate! Afterwards, they cleaned him up and gave him a ride down to the Henries towards Visiting. Since he was scraped up pretty badly and his clothes were torn, he first stopped into Medical. I'm told that after the visit, his father called an attorney. The official report was much different. In conversation with other inmates, it was clear that the Tom Foolery with the golf cart had been going on for some time. It remains a classic example of idle hands being the devil's workshop. As my grandpa used to say, "One boy's a boy; two boys be half a boy, and three boys be no boy at all."

Chapter 21

Cease and Desist

*A hero is an ordinary individual
who finds the strength to persevere and endure
in spite of overwhelming obstacles.*
Christopher Reeve

Building Trades and NCCER

In the spring of 2014, through the direction of our inmate council, we started to explore the idea of creating a vocational program in CUA. All of the literature and information I had read spoke of the value of vocational Education to incarcerated people. A high school diploma is a nice start but that qualifies you for a $9 per-hour job working at McDonalds. (No offense Ray Kroc). There already existed two vocational programs at CUCF, Building Trades and Culinary Arts, both offered by Snow College, a junior college located in a small town about 20 minutes away. Qualifying for either of those opportunities was difficult. Our hope was to provide a wider variety of opportunities to as many inmates as possible.

In our inmate council, we hashed out the beginning details and I set about putting together a grant proposal for the addition of our own building trades program. We have a small yard to the west of our corridor where we already host a garden and herbology class. First we had to get permission from the warden. He thought it was a great idea. We would need tools and building materials, and we would need an instructor. The grant process was relatively simple and once funded, we hired an instructor and set our hands to the plow.

The program was a great success. We used it as an incentive to encourage inmate to improve their TABE scores. To be eligible for the program, TABE scores had to be above 9.0. We would make exceptions to that rule, but it proved to be a great motivator to helping inmates improve.

The first year we had more than 100 participants. Some would start and complete several courses and others continued to participate in everything we offered. We partnered with an organization called NCCER and started to offer certifications in everything from OSHA/Safety to residential electrical. We had inmates who had been contractors on the streets volunteer their time to instruct and supervise. We used the yard and built a small shop and building platform. We were building sheds that we would sell in the local communities. Then we expanded to lawn furniture, beehives, picnic tables and shooting tables. We would sell the products for our cost plus 10% to help us buy tools.

The program grew for three years with no security problems of any kind and no other issues. Then came the order, "Cease and Desist." For reasons I have yet to be made privy to, we were ordered to halt the program. The one and only reason I was given was that in someone's opinion we were exploiting inmates for our profit. HUH? No one was making a profit. Inmates were learning vital employability skills. Inmates were gaining self-worth by building things with their hands, working with other inmates and providing a service to the communities. We had a long waiting list of inmates who wanted to participate. All that the UDC could see were similarities depicted in the movie "Shawshank Redemption." In their minds we were coercing inmates to do things for our own profit. In their minds, inmates were engaged in providing slave labor for our evil purposes.

I was not happy. I went to the warden's office to find out what was going on. The previous warden that had given me permission to build the program had retired and the new warden had no answers. In the transition between wardens, control of Programming had been taken from local control through the warden and given to bureaucratic authority in Salt Lake City, a change that made it nearly impossible for us to be successful. I called and visited and discussed until I was blue in the face, but as I always found in previous experience, there is no arguing with the UDC. The highly successful building trades program was gone. That meant that not only were the inmates denied an amazing opportunity that cost the UDC $0.00 but I had to help our instructor who I had recruited to come in and teach, find a new job. Thankfully that was possible.

They didn't care that I had received grants from the state for which I was accountable. They didn't care that they were pulling a very popular and successful program. They didn't care about the inmate opportunities. No one in the administration of the UDC would listen. I called everyone I knew. I called a state legislator. I emailed the Lt. Governor. Nothing! It was apparent no one cared.

Code Camp

In 2014 my son Dave called me and was excited to enroll in boot camp. (At least that's what I heard). "NO WAY!" I responded. In 2005 my oldest son Josh had decided to join the National Guard and spent the most miserable summer of his life in Fort Sill, Okla. He had been there about five weeks when we got a call at 1 a.m. our time. Josh had been admitted to the base hospital with a severe case of pneumonia. They were calling to inform us of that fact. Later that evening, around 3 a.m., another call came informing us that Josh was being flown to Oklahoma City to the medical center there as his lung had collapsed and he needed a pulmonary specialist. The short story is that we spent 12 days in Oklahoma City getting Josh the medical help he needed and getting him out of the military. Sparing you the rest of the story, it was a miserable experience for all of us. Thus my "NO WAY" response to another boot camp.

What I didn't understand is that he was talking about a computer coding boot camp, an intense 10-week course in which he would spend 50-60 hours a week working with 20 or so other students and a series of coding mentors in order to learn the skills of computer coding.

After some investigation, Dave decided to enroll. To make a long story short, 13 weeks later he had a great paying job writing computer code. He has remained in that field since. It is a wide-open opportunity available to anyone with good intelligence, good problem-solving skills, and a good amount of determination.

Within a short period of time, my mind went to the possibility of implementing a code camp within UPrep. My experience told me that we would have no trouble identifying inmates with the prerequisite skills necessary to be successful. I went to the warden who had given me permission to start the Building Trades course. He thought it was worth a try.

After gaining permission, I wrote a grant to get some needed equipment and software and went to work. Come to find out, I did not originate the idea of coding boot camps inside prisons. Having identified one called The Last Mile in San Quentin Prison in California, I contacted them and they provided me with some excellent insights into the process. At the time, they had been providing a coding academy service to inmates for about 4 years. From them, we were able to shortcut the creation process.

By fall of that year, with help from my son and several inmates, we developed a computer-driven learning tool. We recruited a small group of inmates to start the process and had added that to our UPrep curriculum. All was going as planned. We had a lot of work to do but it was falling in to place. Then came another "Cease and Desist" order.

184

The warden who had given me permission had retired and the "chain of command" for me had moved from local control to Salt Lake City. The newly appointed Director of Programming for the UDC had learned of our efforts and had demanded we halt all operations. I was dumbfounded. Not again.

Like the Building Trades Program, they didn't want us doing anything outside the norm.

I called everyone I knew. I was not interested in losing another valuable program before we even got it off the ground. Thankfully, Stephanie Patton at the State Board of Education, who was a fantastic advocate and support throughout the last half of my tenure, called the right people and a meeting was called to find some way forward. At least we could voice our objections to shutting down our program before it even got started.

I traveled to The Ivory Tower, the UDC admin building in Draper. There, in a conference room we met with 14 people from the UDC. All but two were dressed in uniform. The two without uniforms were the persons in charge of the computer networks throughout the UDC, called (BIT) and one of the deputy directors of the UDC.

I presented my case. Then the majority of the people around the table voiced their opinion. There was little in favor as most disagreed with teaching any computer skills. In their minds, if we taught inmates about computers, (the skills we wanted to teach were how to build websites), the world would come to an end. Someone in that meeting mentioned something about hell freezing over before .... However, when we got to the deputy director and the guy from BIT, the tune changed. In a nutshell, they thought it was a viable, valuable program that should be implemented. In fact, the guy from BIT said, "This is an excellent idea!"

Success!!!

I was dumbfounded and excited. We could continue. With that agreement, and a three-month delay, (it took three months to call the meeting) we were back on track.

That was in the fall of 2017. By February 2018, we had launched our first full-fledged Brickhouse Code Camp Course. Everything prior to that had been experimental and preliminary. Now we had a defined, well-outlined, effective path to teaching coding to inmates. Most of the process was computer-generated instruction that allowed individuals to work at their own pace. We had launched a revolutionary new, self-directed learning tool to teach computer coding inside the prison. We were excited!

The program differed from The Last Mile, used in San Quentin, in that they used live instruction and civilian direct interaction with inmates. That was not something we wanted to venture into either because of the complex logistics or because of the cost.

Then came the Director of Programming with a new "Cease and Desist" order. According to him, we had only been given permission to explore the idea, not implement. Again, another roadblock.

After several weeks of discussion with the parties who had attended the meeting, the Director of Programming came to realize that we weren't out of line. We were allowed to continue. (Are you starting to see a trend?) Brickhouse Code Camp is still going as I write this. However, I still worry every day of receiving another Cease and Desist Order. You see, one of the conditions of that meeting and the grant I received was that there would be a Memorandum of Understanding (MOU) signed between the UDC and UPrep that ensured the UDC would support the program and not undermine it or cancel it. Though I pushed every month for more than a year, Corrections never presented an MOU. An MOU is a 3-4-page document outlining each party's responsibilities. I drafted several options for their approval. None were ever approved.

UPrep

At the time – the spring of 2018 – UPrep was going full speed. We had nearly 300 enrolled students. We taught classes from basic study skills to Math 1050. We had accredited courses from two local community colleges and were providing 15 different courses including Brickhouse Code Camp.

The nature of each of these courses is that they were inmate driven. Inmates acted as instructors. In the case of the college courses, they were proxy instructors who worked as stand-ins for the professor. We would convey information back and forth through one of our secretaries. Professors would provide video instruction, PowerPoint presentations, and lecture notes. The inmate "facilitator" would then take that material and present it to the class. Assignments would be given and gathered and returned to the professors for evaluation. We had created a modified distance learning process that was very effective, efficient, and extremely cost effective. What had started with Weber State University had come to involve Salt Lake Community College and Snow College. I had been fortunate to find in each of these institutions eager and supportive people who saw great value in what we were doing.

In addition, we had made arrangements through Snow College to have an inmate be the actual professor for a business class. The inmate had a master's degree in business and qualified to be an adjunct professor. Snow College officials came in and interviewed him and deemed him a viable candidate to be an adjunct professor non-gratis. We finally had UPrep growing and thriving and then, guess what?

Then came the inevitable. I received notice that the UPrep program, that had run without incident for over 5 years, had to be cut back. The concerns were: 1). Not enough security staff in place. They were now going to require one officer for every 30 inmates. (That would be the only place in the prison, that any of us were aware of, with such a requirement). We had one officer for about 80 inmates. Since all of the courses occurred after hours and on Fridays and Saturdays, the number of available officers was limited. 2). We would have to staff UPrep with a faculty member, something that we had never done as it had not been part of the original agreement. Since UPrep occurred in the off hours, evenings and Fridays and Saturdays, the UDC maintained that inmates could not be trusted to successively execute such a process without staff supervision. That was in spite of the fact that it had occurred very successfully for more than five years without a hitch. As a result, we would be limited to 30 inmates per hour, about one-third of our original number. In addition, we would have to find Education staff willing to work their days off. (Are you starting to see a trend?)

The need for a staff member on site was ridiculous. The programs were directed and administered by qualified inmates. Our required staff member would have nothing to do. They basically come, sit in the administration area and do their homework or whatever. We affectionately referred to them as "the hostage."

I was in total disbelief. So much for the entire second half of their mission statement. So much for the goals and purpose of the ASCENT initiative. Ironically, this time, the directive did not come from the Programming Director. It came from the local warden. The captain in charge of Education security was likely the main culprit. He hated our program and worked overtime to undermine our efforts. The Programming Director, who had issued all the previous cease and desist edicts, had, thanks to the newly appointed Executive Director, actually tried to help us out by providing an extra officer for about 4 months so we would have the staff to host UPrep until the warden could come up with a solution. However, when it was clear that the warden and local security was not going to step up and take care of the security piece, the Programming director had to pull out.

As a result, UPrep currently consists of a diluted version of Brickhouse Code Camp and a few random classes we moved to a couple of the housing units.

Maybe it is me that doesn't get that I don't get it, but why would this happen? None of these programs cost a single dime to the UDC. They had to provide security, something they did at the onset. Even with the requirement of an additional officer for the Friday/Saturday courses, it would cost them less than $12,000/year, a small sum to pay for the opportunities we were providing. I keep wondering how a 70% failure rate is not worth taking a chance with a free and proven program. Even though I believe most of Corrections is made up of good people, they don't seem to realize that applying a Band-Aid on a femoral artery isn't' going to stop the hemorrhage.

If you continue to do what you've done, you'll continue to get what you've got. And, people that don't get it don't get that they don't get it.

After working for six months on a solution and attending several meetings organized by the Utah State Office of Education with the UDC, I came to realize that I had done all that I could do.

Stick a fork in me, I was done. A piecemeal solution to the lack of Corrections in the UDC is not working and will not work. It's going to take a new look, a fresh look. I'm not sure they will ever be able to see the forest for the trees.

I had hoped that the recently appointed Executive Director would see things differently. I think his heart is in the right place. But my conversations with him as well as actions, and public statements made by him tell me that he is still a very long way from any type of real solutions. The trees are so thick, he still can't see the forest. All the right answers to all the wrong questions.

Chapter 22

Visiting

In everyone's life, at some time, our inner fire goes out.
It is then burst into flame by an encounter with another
human being. We should all be thankful
for those people who rekindle the inner spirit.

Albert Schweitzer

The highlight of any inmate's life is a visit from someone from the streets. Though a family member or close friend is preferred, any visit is fantastic. At CUCF the visiting area is fairly occupied during the weekends. During the weekdays, not so much so.

One of our tutors in Education was taking care of his responsibilities, enjoying the day. Out of the blue, an officer told him he had a visitor and his face lit up. He headed out the Education corridor and across the hallway to visiting. You'd think he had received his date and was headed for the gate.

Recently I had occasion to visit Don, an inmate employee of mine for nearly 8 years currently housed in Purgatory. In January of 2019, like most inmates trying to improve themselves, get along, and be productive, he was IPP'd out to county jail. I had occasion to be in St. George and thought I'd drop in. Come to find out, Purgatory doesn't allow in-person visits. The visits are via the prison systems version of Skype. I sat down at the kiosk and entered the required information and Don was called to the monitor. I'll never forget the look on his face as he sat down and recognized me. It was like a little kid at Christmas. Bright eyed and bushy tailed. It wasn't necessarily me; it was the visit.

During the last five years or so of my tenure at the prison, we had more and more visits from groups interested in the positive things we were doing at CUA. Two or three times a year, the state's adult Education program directors would meet and discuss policy, best practices, etc. As our program at CUA grew from just over 200 students to over 800, then over 1,000, the powers that be in the State Board of Education (USBE) asked me to present some of the innovations and changes we had made. At one meeting I presented the idea of mandatory education for any under-achieving inmate. At another I presented the curriculum we had created; over 40 titles for secondary education and nearly as many for our post high school UPrep program. At a different meeting I showed them our SIS system and explained how, if they chose to use it in the Draper prison and jails, it could be easily implemented and used to track and improve student success.

All of these ideas were well received. Over time, the majority of the directors of rural adult education programs, both for the community and the jails, requested and received a full set of the curriculum we had developed for the secondary level education.

Many of these directors were curious to see our program in action and scheduled a visit to CUCF to witness firsthand the changes we had made. Over the next few years, we had over 20 visits from groups of one to five people. Everyone was extremely impressed. The look on their faces was not dissimilar to Don's when I stopped in to visit him. Most left with good ideas, a desire to implement new processes into their programs, and resources to do so.

I invited everyone who would listen to come to see what we were doing. It was revolutionary and I felt that the more people who could see it, the more traction we could gain and the better we could do.

One day the Lieutenant Governor came to CUCF for a visit. He had been asked to speak at a monthly forum organized by and offered to inmates. Knowing he would be in the facility, I ventured in to see if I could get his ear. At the conclusion of the forum, I walked up and introduced myself, gave a brief outline of CUA and invited him to visit Education just down the hall. He was cordial and accepted my offer.

Once there, I gave him the tour. I showed him the tutor room, the print room, the curriculum we had created, the building trades program we had started, (it was still operational at the time) and the beginnings of our computer coding program. Like all our visitors, he was very impressed. He asked what he could do to support us and I suggested maybe a small sum to get the computer coding processes under way. He gave me a very enthusiastic yes. After about 30 minutes and answering all his questions, he left with a promise to follow up. As was typically the case, I could see in his face he was impressed and that he saw value in our program.

Several months later, I scheduled an appointment to meet with the Lt. Governor in his office in Salt Lake City. I had prepared a presentation on prison reform and the value of education in the process. He was gracious and welcomed us into his office. Once there, knowing his time commitments, I jumped right in. Things were going well until I mentioned IPP. You may recall that the IPP program, a pet project of the Governor, was designed to support the building of county jails across the state. I suggested that the IPP program was the antithesis to reducing recidivism. The mood quickly changed. I had made a grave mistake. Though I didn't understand at the time, I had unintentionally attacked a project that was not going to be compromised.

As I concluded my presentation, we were graciously excused and despite multiple follow-ups on my part, with the exception of a response from one of the Lt. Governor's aides, I have not heard from him since. That experience taught me the sacred nature of the IPP program.

My invitations went to the UDC administration as well. Around year four of my tenure, the UDC hired a new Programming director. As soon as he was announced, I invited him to see our program. His responsibilities were for Programming in the prisons and jails throughout the state. It was not uncommon for him to visit CUCF in the normal course of his responsibilities. The main Programming corridor is adjacent to the Education corridor and I had asked the Programming Captain to let me know when the new director would be in the facility. I assumed he would want to stop by and take a tour; everyone else wanted to. Multiple visits to CUCF and a year went by and except for a three-minute introduction, he failed to step a foot inside Education. The second year went by with the same outcome. I might add that multiple times I had invited the then Executive Directors to visit. Again, they would often come to graduation but always declined an invitation to walk the 50 feet to the Education Corridor to visit our program.

Their disinterest was discouraging. The ASCENT program had come and gone with no positive change. Our building trades program had been dismantled with no real reason given. The Computer Coding Program had been canceled and then allowed and then canceled and then once again allowed. It was clear that though the adult education programs throughout the state saw great value in what we were doing, the UDC didn't. Up to that point, with the exception of the annual graduation ceremony, I seldom saw UDC leadership.

That started to change in year seven. The Programming Director seemed to change his tune. I'm not sure what happened but one day he showed up in my office and in his own way expressed his regret for not getting on board sooner but that I now had his full support. A new Executive Director had been appointed and after multiple letters from inmates, word got to him that perhaps something of value was going on in CUA and he started to pay attention. That was encouraging but the support, though well-meaning was limited and slow in coming.

The final indicator of whether the UDC truly supports any Education program within the prison system or not came in the spring of 2019. The Director of Prison Education at the state Board of Education (USBE), Stephanie Patton, a very fine person, an outstanding administrator and a great supporter of all the efforts across the state, determined to host a daylong symposium to showcase all the Education programs throughout the prison system. She had coordinated with the UDC and hosted the symposium at the Fred House Academy, a facility in Draper next to the "Ivory Tower." The purpose of the gathering was to showcase all the different Education programs to the administration and leadership of the UDC in hopes of creating a more coordinated effort towards reform.

I arrived at the facility and recognized representatives from all the various organizations that provide educational services to inmates. There were reps from the University of Utah, Davis Tech Center and Salt Lake Community College. In addition, there were people from the prison schools in Draper, South Park, people from UDOWD, representatives from several county jails, and of course myself, representing CUA. Most of us knew each other well as we had often worked together to provide valued services.

All of the UDC leadership had been invited as had several political figures. To my surprise there were only two sergeants and the Programming Director from the UDC side. The purpose of our gathering was to better coordinate and expose our programs to the UDC. The representatives of the various programs in attendance knew each other well. We didn't need to spend time amongst ourselves any more than we already had.

The meeting started and the first presenters were the two sergeants. They made a presentation about one of the programs provided by the Davis Technology Center. After their 20-minute presentation, they headed for the door. The Director of Programming was already gone. The entire rest of the meeting was conspicuously absent of any UDC personnel.

I felt very bad for Stephanie, who had orchestrated the event. She had worked hard and had high hopes of making some valuable connections. To me, despite recent attempts by the UDC to improve relations and connections, it was what one would expect. It was clear that, to the UDC, the many programs that attempt to make a difference as outlined in their own mission statement were irrelevant and a complete waste of time and money.

So much for the excitement of visiting.

Chapter 23

What happened to my boy?

*Your son will hold your hand for a little while,
but your heart for a lifetime.*
Anonymous

I had been "down" about three years when, while walking in the Education corridor, I looked ahead and saw two beautiful young men walking towards me. It was clear they were brothers. Each was 6'5" walking tall and straight. Their handsome golden-brown faces stood out against the white cloth of their prison uniforms. They were lean and graceful walking into the Education corridor but their eyes, though stark and bright, were full of sadness. They carried their 250-pound muscular frames with ease and even a flash of confidence. Each looked like King Kamehameha the Great, likely the most recognized of Hawaiian leaders who had united the Islands of Hawaii in the late 1700's. If you were to place a chiefly headdress on each and the appropriate attire, both of these young men could fit the part. I watched as they entered the Education secretary's office and inquired about education. Like all inmates at Gunnison, they had been made aware of the education requirements and were there to inquire about their educational responsibilities. Listening to them, they were polite and respectful. Their voice and mannerisms, though regal, were extremely humble.

Finishing their paperwork, they made their way to the testing center and within about an hour, less time than most, finished their required TABE testing. I was curious how they each had done and as I watched them leave the Education corridor, made my way to the testing center to make inquiry. I was not surprised to find that both had passed all three, Reading, Math and Language, with scores of 12.9, near perfect scores.

What had happened to these two boys? How could such potential have gone so far astray? That was a question I had asked myself many times over the previous several years and would ask many times hence. I was told that these two, while being initiated into a gang, had been required to kill someone. They had been caught and were both serving 25 to life. It was heartbreaking.

One of the features of prison that most surprised me was that very thing. I had come expecting to see a "typical" criminal. Someone from the inner city. Someone who wasn't all that smart. Someone with a dumb and sinister nature, kind of like Horace and Jasper, the villains from *101 Dalmatians*. Or possibly the other side of the spectrum, someone like Hannibal Lecter from *Silence of the Lambs*. What I hadn't expected is finding people, many of them young, who were not a whole lot different from the hundreds of basketball players I had worked with over the years. In fact, along those lines, I actually became reacquainted with a man, now an inmate, who 25 years before had served as my basketball manager, and another inmate whose brother I had coached some 20 years earlier. Along with those were several other boys who had attended the high school where I had once taught. I also made acquaintance with several of the more notorious criminals in Utah's history, individuals whose horrendous stories I had learned about on the evening news. On at least two of those situations, I found these men to be likeable people with a gentle and kind side.

What had happened to these men who seemed to have so much potential? What turn in the road had brought them to this point? Having four sons of my own, I tried to imagine what I would do or how I would feel if I found myself sitting in a court room listening to terrible things they had done. I couldn't imagine needing to visit them in prison. The thought literally brought tears to my eyes. What a heartache that must be! What a sense of failure must accompany that mother or father. The Education corridor was across the hall from the visiting area and it was not uncommon as I passed that way to look in and see one of these "boys" being visited by their mother or father or both.

I have had occasion to visit several of the mothers and families of some of the men I met and worked with in prison. Each mother had the same look and feel. They were at peace but full of anguish. They were proud and strong yet humble and somewhat broken. They felt great pain but could display great empathy. There could be few things worse than having to watch your son travel such a terrible road.

Because of what they've done, it is easy to forget that most of these men have families that have been left behind. Every person in there is someone's son or husband or father. It is easy to lose sight of the fact that, in spite of what they have done, they are still people in need of help, love and support.

Below are excerpts from some of the mothers' stories as they related them to me:

"Embarrassment, frustration, fear because you don't have any say, you don't know what to expect, helplessness."

"After the initial shock wears off then the embarrassment sets in. I think that would happen no matter the reason your loved one is arrested. Law enforcement will tell you nothing. The officer who took my son away wouldn't tell me anything. He just gave me a card with a phone number on it. I don't think I even called it. It's funny that the news gets the info but not the family."

"For me, knowing that there's a power greater than mine in my Heavenly Father, I prayed a lot for our son, for our family for His will do be done. I've come to know that He knows best so each prayer was just that this is what I'd like but You know best."

"You worry for their safety."

"For me I would sometimes just be angry. Angry at my son, angry at the victim and family, angry at the judicial system. Anger seemed better than fear. I felt more control for some reason. I really didn't have more control and in the long run, anger will beat you down physically, mentally and emotionally."

"I think the hardest part of it all is the unknown. The judge hands down a 5-to-life sentence and you just don't know how long it will really be. Before our son received his parole date after serving for 3 and a half years we just didn't know how long he would serve. After each visit I would feel sad wondering on the long drive home how much longer he would be there.

"Our son was lucky. He has had some amazing people helping him on his journey. He still does. We all need a little help now and then and he has had that. There isn't a lot of real help available in the system."

"We've had our son home now for six months. It seems longer for some reason. He spent almost five years in prison. I still worry. He's doing amazing, but I still worry. I worry for him; I so want him to have a happy ending. He's doing all he can to obey the conditions of his parole but I think once you're on their radar, law enforcement, you're always checking behind you."

If you remove the drug and alcohol additions, most of these felons are "normal" people. They have families who have a life. It is a challenge, sometimes even for the families, to look past the terrible things they have done and help them change. Though some won't change, we must identify and help the many who will.

Chapter 24

I'm not fit for prison

*The only person you will become
is the person you decide to be.*

Ralph Waldo Emerson

One day as I sat in my office having a discussion with our inmate council, one of the inmates, Don, made the statement, "I'm no longer fit for prison." His remark surprised me and I sat in silence thinking on the matter. At length, I came to agree with his statement.

I first met Don seven years prior. At the time, he definitely needed prison. He was a criminal. He had been a tutor for CUA for several years prior to my arrival. He had worked for a teacher who left just one year after my assignment to CUA because, well, it was for the best. He left to work at a local high school. Anyway, back to Don, he was running a store from the stuff he could "garner" from Education; pencils, pens, card stock, paper, notebooks. He later told me how some of the tutors would hide stuff in the suspended ceiling tiles and then retrieve it later to barter with.

Interestingly, Don had been a part of our inmate council from nearly the beginning. You may recall that I had a meeting early on with the tutors explaining that things were gonna change and that I did not hire criminals. Shortly after that, I had to fire several of Don's buddies. I called him into my office to help him understand that he had a choice; change or leave. I am very thankful that there was enough good inside Don that he chose to change and stay with Education.

Over those next seven years that he worked for us, Don become a fine man. Over time, he became the lead tutor in our tutor room. He had great insight into the prison system – the way inmates think, what is needed for an inmate to change, and the process of coming to oneself. Mostly though, along with me, he had seen the evolution of CUA from its feeble beginnings through the creation of the Outreach program, the growth created by the implementation of our Student Information Systems and adaptations, and the development of UPrep.

More than anyone else, he knew our systems and the reason for our rules and processes. He had become a trusted friend who I knew I could rely on. I had made several other trusted compatriots over the years. All had stories similar to Don's. All the others had been 'rolled up' and sent to county when Officer Johnson realized that I placed a lot of trust and responsibility in them. For some reason he had overlooked Don, at least until now (January of 2019).

Back to his statement, "I'm not fit for prison." As a staff, including inmates, we loved to tackle problems. However, this time we had no solution. He may no longer be fit for prison, something with which I would completely agree, but there was nothing we could do about it. This time the problem lay with the system, and the Board of Pardons.

I don't want to be critical of a group I don't even know. From where I sit, it appears that, like most of the Corrections system personnel, the Board of Pardons is made up of good people caught in a terrible system. They are expected to go through an information packet, have a brief interview with an inmate and determine if he is fit for parole. It is a crapshoot at best. There isn't a person alive who could do that effectively.

Within our conversations in the inmate council we regularly posed the question, "Why does one inmate get paroled and another doesn't?" There was never any rhyme or reason. It is a common question posed within all aspects of the system, inmate, security staff, and volunteer. I would further pose the question, "Why do we let any inmate out of prison who is unchanged or perhaps changed for the worse and is almost 100% certain to either violate parole or reoffend after being released?"

It was about at this time that I heard on the news the story of a recently released felon who had stolen a car, abducted a girl and killed a police officer all within several days of his release from prison. Clearly something is terribly wrong with the system. Though this example is more dramatic than most, similar occurrences are not uncommon.

The problem, as I see it, is that all of Corrections is trying to move forward from a prison system without any real change except in name. The question, "Why do we let anybody out of prison who is unchanged or changed for the worse and is almost 100% likely to reoffend after they leave?" is a valid one. That was a question asked as well by all the business leaders who participated with us on the ASCENT committee. Incidentally, it was also a question posed by the original ASCENT Proposal.

A constant echo I hear over and over again in the current system is that no inmate should be allowed in any serious program until they are less than a year or two from the gate. In the current system, inmates sit in a cesspool absorbing the crap of prison until about a year left, then Corrections makes the feeble effort to pull them out while still in the cesspool, clean them off, deodorize them and teach them everything they need to know to have a successful life. Here I would refer the reader to "The Violin Story."

It's like parents who have a child. They let him run wild until 16. He can come and go as he pleases, he can make whatever choice he wants. He can do whatever he wants, have any friend he would like. Then, at 16 the parents try to rein him in and prepare him for life. He must now toe the line. He must now be responsible. He must now be accountable. No sane parent in the world takes that approach. Yet that is exactly the approach of the UDC.

The goal should be to allow men to change so that they are "no longer fit for prison." There needs to be a path to follow that leads to responsibility, accountability, service, purpose and hope. This process should last the entire term of their sentence. I believe that to be eligible for parole after a minimum sentence of say five years, an inmate must spend five years pursuing a path of rehabilitation. If they want to be idiots for 5 years, their clock is still at 0. If they would be eligible for parole after, say, 10 years, they need to spend 10 years on that rehabilitation path. If they have a 10-year sentence and choose to do nothing for four years and then go to work creating real change, their minimum sentence would be 14 years. In addition, each potential parolee would be required to move up the ladder, so to speak. No inmate would be eligible for parole until he has moved up the ladder and has been living in ASCENT's Tier 5 for at least a year. (Refer to Chapter 29)

The STRIVE program in the Gale housing unit pursues such a philosophy. They look to start the change in inmates as soon as possible and keep it as long as possible. According to their current Gale Captain, they boast a recidivism rate less than 10% for offenders leaving the facility from the Gale housing unit. That is more than noteworthy. Their process of self-selection and self-directed behavior works even without a real systemwide buy-in by Corrections.

Unfortunately, and perhaps predictably, it is not uncommon for the STRIVE program to face the same challenges from the UDC that we do in Education. IPP constantly takes inmates out of STRIVE for county jail. There was a time when the STRIVE Captain was constantly working to prevent his program from being eliminated. In general, the UDC sees no value in STRIVE. It is very frustrating.

I had been "down" for eight years; we were having great success in our Education programs because we have expected and enacted real change. While all the inmates we worked with have not changed, some have. Those who had changed were moving towards being 'no longer fit for prison."

Yet this is only a small part of a much larger puzzle. As part of our inmate councils, we put together a tiered program for individual inmates to earn the right to parole. We did this during the time I sat on the Education and employment ASCENT committee. We developed it for the committee and it was well-accepted by the majority of the group until Captain Train Wreck came on the scene.

This tiered program is still just a rough draft and is included in Chapter 29. The fact that it was created with the help of inmates is an indication to me that it is very do-able, although with some needed modification.

I hope you'll read through it under the "A Real Solution," Tier Program chapter of this book.

This is a writing from Inmate Edmond, who was the key element in the beginning of our CUA/Outreach program. I came to know Edmond as we were introduced and he presented many of the base ideas of the Education system we established inside CUCF. He worked tirelessly to produce a system of Education in CUCF that would actually be of benefit to its recipients. This story connects with the "My Sentence" chapter of this book.

At first the sentencing matrix of 101 months wasn't really too much of a concern for me. I still had faith in what my defense attorney had told me and believed that the most I would receive from the BOPP was an additional 18 months or so. I entered the original hearing with the utmost confidence knowing that I had completed my original mapping at least twice over. I had earned my high school diploma. I completed the yearlong HOPE substance abuse treatment program, I participated in an additional year of one-on-one weekly therapy sessions with my HOPE therapist, I had successfully completed countless other classes and courses related to thinking and behavior modification, I assisted by leading the creation of the CUA/Outreach Education program and I was a model inmate who had never received any kind of disciplinary action.

I felt like I was perfect in my rehabilitation. I didn't have any substance abuse relapses. I hadn't been in a fight or assaulted anyone. I didn't have a single mishap that would suggest that I needed more incarceration to reform or rehabilitate myself. I took full accountability and maximized my efforts to change my life so that I could never, ever again be described as the person described in my presentencing report. From two weeks after my initial arrest I got to work on myself and developed a contrite spirit and a broken heart. I was absolutely unequivocally ready to be released back into society after serving four-and-a-half years. I had made amends with those most affected by my crimes and was ready to resume my role as father to my four children and provider to my family. I was sure that I had checked all the boxes for mitigating my sentence.

My original BOPP hearing lasted fifty-five minutes. I am told that is much longer than most hearings. I was seen by a hearing officer, not a board member, which is fairly standard. The process went as I was told it would. At the completion of the interview, the officer said, "It would be a copout for the board not to give you a release date."

It took several weeks to get the decision back from the BOPP. It came via inmate mail. When I opened it and saw the decision for a rehearing in June of 2020, I was dumbfounded.

A week or so later I was notified that I owed just over $15,000 in restitution and was given a statement that had mitigating and aggravating circumstances checked off as a *rationale for the BOPP's decision. By them, I was considered a "person of trust" and "the main instigator of a group." Neither was true at the time of my crime. I worked as a building contractor, not a person of trust and I acted alone in my crime. Even now, five years later, no one has ever been able to explain any of it to me. Not Corrections, not the BOPP, not my caseworkers, not my attorney. The only justification I have received over the years is that I have a 101-month matrix and the board is intending that I serve the entire amount.*

I watch as other inmates who have done the least amount of work rehabilitating themselves parole well before their matrix and I have to ask why?

I could take pages and list all I have done, the classes I have taken, my critical service provided in the beginning of the education revolution outlined in this book, the Programming courses I have tutored, mostly the change that has occurred inside me. Suffice it to say that as Mark would say, "I am no longer fit for prison" and am doing no one any good where I am.

Don't get me wrong, I'm not suggesting that what I did was justified, excusable, or that I had a good reason for doing it. It wasn't and I don't. I know because of my rehabilitation that I could have handled things in a much more appropriate way, saving myself from incarceration and allowing me to save my daughter from another six years of similar abuse.

Looking back, I had a traumatic childhood, to say the least. Because of abuse in my home, I left home at 14 years of age. Finding my way to Utah, I started at McDonalds working my way up to manager. Then I started a very successful construction business building and remodeling homes on the East Bench of Salt Lake. It was at that point, lacking any real bearings of appropriate behavior that most people get from their childhood, that I lost focus, started "living the high life," and ruined the lives of those I love most.

At the age of 35, I threw away a very successful life.

Being self-determined by nature, I chose from the very beginning of my incarceration to "fix what ailed me." Thus the great efforts I have taken to be involved in any valuable and often not valuable class and course offered by the UDC. Had I left it up to Corrections, I'm afraid that I would likely leave this experience worse off than I was when I got here. That is the case with the large majority of men who enter prison.

The BOPP agreed to provide me a rehearing which was scheduled for November 2018. The hearing was held February 2019. Going into the hearing, I was very hopeful I would receive an immediate release.

However, the hearing wasn't what I expected. The officer, different from the last time, was cold and clearly lacked the kindness and compassion of my previous BOPP officer. In spite of pleas by my two oldest daughters for release, the outcome was not as expected. They posted my release date as June 1, 2021, an additional 27 1/2 months.

This time the rationale for the decision said that my risk or behavior warranted additional incarceration beyond my sentencing guidelines which flies in the face of everything laid out in the documentation we provided.

Why am I still here? Does the BOPP not have any faith in the Programming and rehabilitation services offered by the UDC? Can it be possible that the UDC and the BOPP have absolutely NO real method to determine or differentiate a reformed offender from an anti-social one? Are there other objectives in play that as a society we are all unaware of? Is it possible that the BOPP is simply abusing their power trying to keep corrected and reformed individuals behind bars? Clearly there are more questions than answers when it comes to the actions and decisions of the BOPP.

*I can honestly say that I am a changed man **in spite** of the UDC. Some time ago I was no longer fit for prison.*

Chapter 25

Rights without Responsibility = Entitlement

Give a man a fish and he will eat for a day.
Teach a man to fish and he will eat for a lifetime.

Anonymous

We live in the greatest country in the history of the world. America is without parallel when it comes to development, human rights, life style, opportunity, inclusion etc., in spite of what many in the media or elsewhere may claim. No country on earth has done more to improve the human condition than the United States of America. No question we have our problems and are not perfect but no country is. Like all things, all people and all nations, there is good and bad. In America, the good we do far outweighs the bad.

Our founding fathers started the idea with a desire to create a "new experiment" type of government, by the people and for the people. Sometimes I wonder if we have lost our way. However, I am sure that the closer we stick to the principles, which are all of a conservative nature of our Founding Fathers, the closer we will come to succeeding.

They started out with the basic rights of life, liberty and the **pursuit** of happiness. Then came the Bill of Rights, all of which expound the three basic rights in the constitution. All of these were made to protect the individual first, as well as the group. They do so very well. The problem comes in the idea of responsibility. That word is never mentioned in the constitution or the Bill of Rights. However, its application is critical for a successful society. One may question why the builders of our nation left it out. My answer is simple. I believe they could not conceive a world of entitlement where no responsibility was present. They knew responsibility was critical to life. Theirs were lives of responsibility. Their sense of responsibility led them to pursue a life developing the rights of others who were much less fortunate but who were also mostly responsible individuals.

We live in a world where we often forget we have a responsibility to help our fellow man. We often forget the responsibility taught in the Bible of the traveler on the road to Jericho.

We also live in a world where many people think someone owes them something. They deserve free health care or they deserve free food or fun or whatever it may be. They believe they should be able to say whatever they want, whenever they want. "It's a free country."

Though all of that is true, they miss the responsibility part. For example, it is not uncommon in our world for people to use extremely poor language. People have the right to do that. However, responsible people use language appropriate for their situation and try not to infringe on the rights of others who may not appreciate such colorful language.

An example of that occurs in sports arenas across the country. I'm a Utah Jazz fan. I've always liked the Jazz. I like to root for the home team. They haven't always been great but nonetheless have had their good years. When my kids were younger, we would at times attend the games. The atmosphere was mostly wholesome. Fans were generally rowdy and aggressive without being vulgar or offensive. Whether we were sitting in the lower bowl or the upper bowl, the fans would yell and support their team and harass the opposition. It was a fun experience.

Last winter, my oldest son bought some tickets for his brothers and I to attend a Jazz game. It had been more than 12 years since our last such adventure. As I sat there it was clear that we were sitting in a section with season ticket holders. Many of them were a little older than me. There were many husbands and wives sitting together in the upper bowl enjoying the game. There were some younger families over to our right and some old codgers across the concourse opening to our left. What I wasn't ready for was the young 20 somethings behind us. Early in the second quarter, probably after the beer had started to work its magic, four or five of them started using every profane word I've ever heard. I was shocked. It would have made a sailor blush. It didn't just happen once and it wasn't just men. I was very disappointed. As we sat through the game, the vulgarity continued. I don't deny that we live in a country that allows freedom of expression. These people had a "right" to scream whatever they wanted. However, personal responsibility and self-respect states that a person should consider the people around them and reserve their poor choice of words and actions for themselves and their friends and protect others from their tirades. Freedom comes at a price and the biggest price is not personal rights, it is personal responsibility. (Just ask anyone in the military). In fact, personal responsibility, not personal rights, is the key to freedom.

I have found that to be the case in prison as well. One can have few rights, but by being personally responsible, one can have freedom. Likewise, one can be completely "free" but without acting responsibly is in bondage at worse and obnoxious at best. Perhaps I should have addressed the behavior and language of those obnoxious fans. I really don't think it would have solved anything; only made it worse. People with no sense of personal responsibility can seldom be helped or corrected – they are entitled.

The prison world is no different from the outside world in this regard. There are some inmates who are responsible and accountable and there are some inmates who are not. The ones who are not responsible have a sense of entitlement that is ugly. They think they deserve a certain freedom or liberty without ever thinking that they would need to earn it. They will complain, for example, when one inmate is allowed to participate in a Level Gain Incentive in which those who earned educational level gains within the past six months are allowed to attend a movie and have an ice cream.

"It's not fair."

I once was told that "fair" is a 4-letter word and that being "fair" to everyone is the most unfair thing one can do. I actually believe that. Life is not fair and the more fair we try to make it, the worse it gets. On the other hand, one reaps what one sows. That is a law of nature. Though the next guy's fields may seem to yield a bigger harvest, and you may think you had to do much more work than your neighbor, if you don't sow, you don't reap.

That brings up the complexity of prison life. A common mantra in prison from the guards is to treat all inmates the same. It is the process of being "fair." That typically happens. The problem is, with some exceptions, an inmate who is a low-life is often treated the same as the inmate that is trying to get along, learn, grow and change. PML levels have improved that process a little. Inmates with higher PML's are often given additional freedoms or opportunities than those with lower levels. However, with the exception of officers who work closely with individuals, all inmates are looked upon by officers as bad, untrustworthy, on the take, criminals, worthless, etc. The ones who are trying to change and are being responsible are constantly pushed back in the primordial ooze by the attending officers. I realize they are inmates and that they live in a prison and that prisons are full of criminals. However, if prisons are ever going to change to Correctional facilities in which a path of real change and real growth is to be facilitated, a paradigm shift is needed.

The inmates who are being responsible, who are making real efforts to eliminate their criminal behavior and who want to become something better must be allowed to do so. That allowance has to come from the system. The system must stop being "fair" and start rewarding responsibility on a day-to-day basis. It must stop throwing the responsible inmates back into the cesspool but start allowing them to rise out of the ooze and make a better life. That includes moving into a more agreeable setting.

This idea of rewarding responsibility is the basis for the tier system we outline in Chapter 29. It would require responsibility on the part of prison administration, prison leadership, prison staff and inmates but would lead to real possibility and hope for change.

With few exceptions, the current prison system does not effectively promote this idea.

Chapter 26

If I were King

We have more power than will;
and it is often by way of excuse to ourselves
that we fancy things are impossible.
Francois Duc De la Rochefoucauld

A number of years ago, the State of Utah set forth the idea of indeterminant sentencing for inmates. In a nutshell, the idea is that for inmates to be released on parole, they have to "accomplish" a set of criteria set forth by the judge. Said criteria is now referred to as an inmate's "matrix." Using this criterion, the board of pardons would then review the inmate's portfolio, if you will, and decide if in fact the inmate is ready to be returned to society. The idea was noble. I would agree with the basic concept. If a person is not fit to live in society because of obvious behavioral issues, returning them to society without some correction seems, well, ill-advised.

The problem with that idea is very obvious – there is no consistency. Any judge is going to do his best to establish to the matrix. Then, even if that could be made consistent, the Board of Pardons is left with a completely impossible task of determination, without seeing the inmate except at a "board hearing." At that hearing one member of the board or often a representative of the board either in person or via closed circuit, interviews the inmate for about 20 minutes to determine readiness for release. They look through the inmate's packet to see what he has done. Really, they look over the packet and see the hoops he has jumped through to get released. An example of that is a current 4-month time cut for a high school diploma. That is, the system allows a 4-month time cut for any inmate that earns his high school diploma while incarcerated. It is ineffective. Let me give you several examples. Suppose two inmates decide they want the 4-month time cut and enroll in school. One needs 1 credit to graduate and the other needs 9. The first can complete the task in a matter of months where the other will take years. There is no indication that either has changed or improved his life, only that he now has a piece of paper that says he graduated. Though it is possible that a genuine, real change took place, the piece of paper is not an indicator. There are many Programming classes that are also required. Once completed, they are added to the inmate's packet. Like a high school diploma, they are not true indicators of real change, only hoop jumping.

Currently, inmates are released with no apparent rhyme or reason. Inmates watch as thugs are let out of prison while others who actually have reformed and learned their lesson remain incarcerated. The UDC is full of problems but by far the greatest problem is found in the Board of Pardons who have the impossible task of selecting who is ready and who is not. I don't blame the people on the board. I would bet they are fine people. They just literally have an impossible task. In the current system, it is not feasible.

As I did my eight years, it was not difficult to identify those inmates who were ready for release. I'm not saying that every person I deemed ready for parole would succeed but it would not be hard, from my position, to identify those who definitely were not ready. That being said, the solution really is not that complicated, at least not from my view.

The general perspective of the UDC is that all inmates are the same. All are criminals. None of them can be trusted. They are all trying to victimize and terrorize. Therefore, just throw them all in the cesspool together and let them rot until a year or so before release then "fix" them and prepare them

214

for society. Sounds ridiculous, right? It is the current system. It is not a reasonable idea.

In conversation with the Executive Director, he describes his huge problem with Transition. That is the part of the parole process that begins when an inmate returns to society. Their AP&P officers' caseloads are overwhelming. However, I don't see Transition as starting when an inmate is released to go back to society. If Corrections would start an inmate's transition the day he or she enters prison, their current problems with transition would be cut dramatically.

The answer lies in creating a system of progression through which inmates desiring to be released beyond their maximum sentence must comply and move through before ever being considered for parole. For example, suppose an inmate has a 5- to 25-year sentence. To be considered for parole, the individual must have progressed through the process to its completion for a minimum of five years and be living above TIER 5 for a minimum of their last year. Over time, inmates, through natural selection, separate themselves so that the ones that do not want to change can be housed together and managed very much as they are now. Whether that be the majority of inmates or just a limited number, they can hang out and do their "thing." However, those who want to change and want a chance for parole must start down a path of self-discovery and change that will eventually lead them to thinking differently, more productively, more positively, on the inside first, then on the outside. The process takes time and effort.

For any of us, change is hard. It requires constant effort. It requires a strong desire and motivation. It requires a plan. I look at my own life and that of nearly every other man I know. My main motivation is my family. I have a strong desire to provide for them and take care of my parental duties and my responsibilities to my wife. Many of those desires to care for them comes from my deep belief in God as my loving Heavenly Father and my desire to please Him and do

His will. These traditions and beliefs come from good parents and extended family that are great people and examples. Though none of us is perfect, we all work, in our own way to be good, productive people. Even with that positive background, improving, growing and changing is difficult. Like most people, every day I look in the mirror and try to demand a little more of myself, to be a little kinder, more considerate and more caring. For my entire life I have been a goal setter. The process is often no longer formal. I try to identify what I want to accomplish and set forth a process of accomplishment. The process changes as progress is made and growth is the result.

The process is the same for any person. First comes the motivation, the why. Then a clear path must be established and worked towards, the what. Third, applying the path and adjusting along the way is the how. These processes are required as moving forward evolves into a better and better plan. Finally, accountability is critical to the process. That accountability comes from self, from family, from friends, from employers, from church leaders, etc. It involves a personal evaluation of the constant two steps forward and one step back process of growth.

Then, of course, comes the reward of success. That is the most interesting part of the process. The way I see it, the most valued outcomes are not the accomplishment itself or the sense of accomplishment achieved but the internal change in self that comes along the path.

It is that personal growth that is most often the greatest reward in any endeavor. That is true for the average, regular person as well as for the inmate in prison. I believe personal growth is an acquired taste that only comes to those who learn the process and practice it over and over again. It is a great and important part of our lives.

So, if I were king, I would require that any felon, once in prison, to be eligible for parole, would be required to voluntarily participate in a self-help program. It would

216

require years to accomplish and they would have to demonstrate a concerted, self-driven, long-term effort of real improvement.

It would be systematic. It would allow inmates, as they accomplish and progress, to move to more desirable living situations. It would require many Corrections officers to serve as mentors and life-coaches. It would require inmates, as they progress, to serve likewise as mentors and facilitators for other inmates working their way up through the system. It would require inmates to live crime-free and live in a crime-free environment for a number of years preparing them to return to a civilized society. Those who chose not to jump on the train and participate could live in a situation similar to the current general population conditions of the prison. They would never be eligible for parole. They would have to serve their entire sentence before being released.

The self-help process would be voluntary, self-selecting and simple to administer.

A properly run prison system is the perfect venue for such a social engineering project. The participants are incarcerated for a reason. Clearly, they struggle with society's minimum expectations. They have victimized others. They have, for whatever reason, crossed lines of acceptable behavior. Now they are incarcerated, having given up their right to freedom. Currently, as it stands, they are simply living in a cesspool of continued crime and illegal activity. Under the existing situation, real change is virtually impossible except for those with the strongest of internal guides. The motivation for change is virtually nonexistent except for those with a strong enough conscience to overcome the negative forces both from Corrections and from other inmates that constantly and persistently drag them down. In the current system there is little hope.

Using existing buildings, housing units, etc., a pathway to progression could be easily followed. Inmates who come to themselves and start to get it will be allowed to, through their efforts and initiative, earn the right to move up in their world. (Sound familiar?) Inmates will be allowed to live in a housing unit fitting their personal level of progress. Those who don't want to change will be housed together. Those who want to work towards a better end will be, after they have completed certain base criteria, given the chance to enter the Tier Program as briefly described in the chapter, "A Real Solution." As they learn new personal skills and work to become better people, they will then be able to move further and further up the ladder. (Sound familiar?) Different housing units represent different Tiers. At times, higher Tiered inmates may choose to live with lowered Tiered inmates as mentors. That would be their choice. Nonetheless, inmates, as they progress, will be able to move out of the primordial ooze they currently live in and step up and become good people.

Realizing that nobody will get it the first time, as inmates fail, they will be sanctioned and or sent back to re-do a Tier. Inmates that fail miserably may be sent back to the beginning or perhaps to the living environment where no change is desired.

For an inmate to be eligible for parole, they must complete their minimum sentence working through the tier system with a minimum of time living in at least Tier 5.

The IPP program that is so feared by inmates could be used as an integral part of the Tier system. There are some jails that currently provide a viable service. Kane County jail, for example, currently hosts several treatment programs that have proven effective. Their jail commander and local sheriff see the value of helping inmates change. They have been innovators in the idea of correction education within the system. A few other jails provide quality educational services and still others provide building trades programs and other effective, innovative opportunities. However, the majority of county jails lack the facilities, interest and motivation to do anything but lock inmates up.

Each jail could, of their own accord and perhaps with help from the state, create a unique opportunity for progressing inmates. Road crews, cabinet shops, computer coding opportunities are all viable and do-able options.

To reward and incentivize the more advanced inmates to want to go to county, each of these qualifying jails could create a JRI proposal associated with their specific program in which participating inmates, through a series of "distance Ed" courses could qualify to have their board hearing date moved up. If done correctly, the IPP program would be just that, a way to place qualified inmates into a Tier program that fits their needs and rewards their efforts to change.

The county jails who don't want to integrate a successful program, could take the incorrigible inmates that have no intent of changing. It may require an additional security fence around the facility. It may necessitate improved security training etc. It would be their choice. In my view, the current system which simply uses inmates to pay the bills rather than helping correct behavior is unacceptable. By doing this, inmates wouldn't simply be moved at random but would be assigned to different programs as they progress through the Tier system.

This process would be simple to start, implement and carry out. It would take the current system in which, more often than not, the tail wags the dog, to a coordinated system designed to, as their name suggests, provide **correction** to wayward individuals. It would require a vision and acceptance by the state legislature to pass laws requiring change in requirements for parole eligibility. It would require the judicial system to use indeterminant sentencing and require compliance and progression through the Tier System to be eligible for parole. It would require a complete paradigm shift in the culture and direction within the UDC. It would make the life of the board of pardons whose current task is impossible, much easier and more consistent. It could be easily started in CUCF and spread to Draper and eventually to the new prison facility west of the airport in Salt Lake City.

I don't think for a minute that all inmates will take advantage of such an opportunity, nor do I believe that all inmates that participate and succeed within the Tier system and eventually parole, will remain on the streets. They won't. I am completely confident however that the current recidivism rate of 70% will be greatly reduced, if for no other reason than the inmates who currently want to change will be separated from ones that don't. Living in a cesspool is no way to "clean up." My experience tells me that as less-committed inmates watch successful inmates leave on parole, many more will decide they want a chance to change and will take the steps necessary to participate in the Tier ASCENT Program.

There would be no real additional cost involved and the process of natural selection will, without a doubt lower the number of returning offenders considering that over 70% of current inmates in Utah are repeat offenders.

The good news is that everyone benefits. The recidivism rate drops dramatically. The system gains credibility. The system starts to make sense. The security staff begin to find fulfillment in their jobs, and officer retention improves. The Board of Pardons no longer has the impossible task of deciding if an inmate is "ready" for release. The current over-population of the prison system is solved. The overburdened AP&P has manageable caseloads. The taxpayer saves millions of dollars on a system that reduces the number of inmates. Society benefits by having better potential parolees. It would finally make sense. If I were King.

Chapter 27

Inmate Edmond's experiences

I would like to include here the final writings of Inmate Edmond on his experience as an inmate in the UDC system. It includes the synopsis of his journey, its ups and downs. It surmises his experiences and the things, positive and negative, he has learned from his incarceration. He includes a brief life sketch and some of the events that led to his incarceration. Mostly it says what needs to be done to create a real Corrections system.

At the end of the day, my family paid the biggest price for my mistakes. I have done time well over my matrix and according to the system, have done my time. When I first was incarcerated I committed to myself to do all that I could to identify my personality flaws and change my thinking and behavior so that I never repeat anything close to my pre-prison crimes.

Currently, my torment is that I have been shelved and warehoused and have had to fight for every opportunity for change. Many of the pieces are there but there is no clear path. All efforts to reform and change are squashed by an antiquated system that has no rhyme or reason. I am to the point that I feel a more and more urgent need to provide the support to my family that they have missed in my absence. What they need is for me to return home so I can actually be present and of use to them. We are just waiting around for the next 18 months to pass so that my family can finally start healing from what I broke so long ago.

Without question I earned the right to be incarcerated. I accepted that reality a long time ago and with that acceptance I committed to positive change. It is so very unfortunate that the current UDC system has been unable to tell my reformed self from the man who was sent to prison over a decade ago. I did all the work. I completed everything they required of me and much more, yet I'm still here. Many others who made almost no effort to change and have effected no change in their lives have been paroled. Why do so many unchanged inmates gain parole? There is no current accurate measure in place to truly identify those who are reformed.

Unfortunately, a lot has changed for all of us. We have all grown weary and exhausted. None of us trust the justice system. Some terrible things have happened to my children in my absence. My family is near destitute and struggling. All these things I could resolve if I were free. I just don't know why I'm still here. There is no method to the madness of the UDC.

Over the years I have learned several important things that I would like to share.

1) We were all victims of something long before we became perpetrators. Most of us learned to act out in violence so violence could no longer be acted out upon us.

2) It takes two things to rehabilitate or reform an offender. First, the removal of internal demons that plague our lives. Second, replacing those with hope and purpose in this life.

3) My success in being rehabilitated or reformed in the current UDC system was a constant uphill battle that I had to create for myself. Corrections only created obstacles and hurdles for me while I tried to find the path. Anyone – officer, volunteer, teacher, principal, etc., who tried to help me or any other offender – is marginalized.

4) *Any additional opportunities at rehabilitation or reform ended the day I was IPP'd out to county jails. There are little to no real opportunities available in the IPP system.*

5) *If it weren't for my first wife, who has been my best friend for 28 years, my children who never lost faith in my ability, my friends who supported me financially and a handful of volunteers and civilian employees at the various facilities, I would have never made this journey. Their belief in me sustained me when I no longer had belief in myself.*

6) *Inmates are a demographic of men who want and need to be accepted, approved of, and loved by society. Though it is the case that we are responsible for our actions, for the most part our acting out began as little children when we stopped receiving these things.*

7) *If you don't know what you want or desire, you will inevitably settle for what you know.*

8) *If our goal as a society is to rehabilitate and reform our criminals, then sending them to jail or prison for correction is the last thing we should be doing unless we are willing to create a rehabilitation program within "Corrections."*

But then again, what do I know? I'm just a ghetto kid from Seattle. At just 14 years of age I ran away to escape the constant onslaught of physical, mental and sexual abuse in my home. I dropped out of school and ran the streets of Seattle amuck. By the time I was 17 I had been shot, was a gang member, had both hands crushed in a cardboard bailer and was headed for jail for theft. My life had become completely unmanageable and I was scared. The only thing that saved me at that time was the love and acceptance of my best friend's dad. He rescued me from the dugout I was living in near his house and said, "Come with me. I'll show you a better way." What he did in that moment was restore my hope and purpose. As a result of following him, I can proudly say that I never stole another thing after that.

Eventually the courts favored me and I had to complete 30 days in a facility or 240 hours of community service. I opted for the community service.   While awaiting my case resolution, I traveled to Salt Lake City. I went with my best friend to visit his mom. That's when I met my first wife and got my first glimpse of how people lived outside the ghetto. The streets were clean, the yards were green and everybody seemed to have a nice house and a new car. I wanted a life like they had. I had hope and purpose.

My visit to Utah changed my life forever. I had fallen madly in love with that girl and decided I needed to finish my community service as quickly as possible so I could get back to her. Once completed, I boarded a Greyhound Bus with two plastic bags of clothes and $10.00 in my pocket. I was 17 years old and getting ready to start my new life. I hired on at two places and worked my butt off. We married about a year later and had a child about 3 years after that. Unfortunately, I ruined it all because of unfaithfulness. My infidelity brought out many of the feelings and experiences of my childhood and five years later I was divorced and remarried to my girlfriend.

My second wife and I had 3 kids over the course of seven years. Our mutual brokenness led to our bonding. I ended up starting a construction company. Financially our lives were great. Everything else, however, was an illusion to cover up the demons of our past. I was incapable of being a good husband and she was incapable of being a good mother. In the end, my dormant rage came alive and I brutally beat her for reasons that really don't matter. Now I'm in prison.

Many parts of my story are very typical of the many men who have had to serve time. There are also many parts of my story that are very unique. I would not classify myself as an above-average human being but I am confident that I have been an above-average inmate. I have never subscribed to the prevalent convict mentality. I don't make excuses for my choices. The biggest difference between myself and most other inmates is that in spite of the broken system, in spite of the constant battles of prison life, I still have hope and purpose in this life. I have something to return to once I'm free of these walls. Another difference is that what you see is what you get. I just need you to take a good look at me.

There are three significant problems with the current incarceration system. The first is that they have no idea how to rehabilitate or reform an individual. That is evident by the simple fact that if they really knew, they wouldn't work so hard to remove any and all hope and purpose from every incarcerated individual. The second problem that is evident is the fact that the current system has absolutely no idea if or when an individual is rehabilitated and reformed. If they did, once the debt to society is paid, they wouldn't keep them incarcerated a single day past successful rehabilitation. And third, we wouldn't let them out of prison until certain levels of rehabilitation are obtained.

All criminals are not created equal. Some have addiction problems. Some have mental health issues. Some have literacy problems. Some have been victims of sexual or physical or mental abuse. Some are gang members, some are not. Some come from wealth, others from poverty. The list goes on and on. Yet the current system has a one-size-fits-all mentality that takes no real effort to provide hope, purpose or change for any of them and they have the gall to call it Corrections.

There is no accurate system of reporting to the BOPP. Without a clear program and path to rehabilitation, the BOPP has no real chance of successfully identifying who is reformed and who is not. It is a crap-shoot at best. Most civilians would find it disheartening to know that the official policy of any of the officers within the UDC is to not comment on an inmate one way or the other as to his level of rehab and his chances of successful parole. They can't give real feedback to the BOPP about an inmate because they feel it creates a security risk for their officers.

What about the security risk to society when unchanged, unreformed inmates are released back into society? Tell me something. Who is better equipped to identify if an inmate is ready for re-entry into society than the men and women who interact with them every day?

No one on the BOPP has every met me. I have been interviewed by a BOPP representative two times in ten years. Those interviews lasted less than an hour. How could they ever really know my state of mind or my ability to succeed on the streets?

We need a true structured, Tiered System that isn't completely arbitrary. We need educators, psychologists and a system that can restore hope and purpose in the inmate's life. Against all odds, I was blessed enough to find that out for myself. In spite of the system, I was strong-willed enough to demand it. Sadly, in the end I was punished and exiled for my efforts. The system does not reward positive change – it rewards continued criminal behavior. It is broken. A broken system will never give broken people any real opportunity to become whole again. The fix is not that complicated. I saw a glimpse of it at CUCF in the STRIVE program as well as in the CUA/Outreach and UPrep programs.

Chapter 28

I'm glad I came to Prison

Of all of the interesting insights I have gained, one is that of the redemption achieved by those inmates who "get it." I'm confident that many of the incarcerated men I have met don't believe they should be in prison. Some deny the charges. Others think their sentence was too harsh. Not many are glad, at least not for the right reason, that they came to prison. However, I believe that when an inmate becomes thankful that they were incarcerated, that is when they start to get it. I'd like to illustrate that with several stories.

The first story is about Reggie. You may remember me referring to him. While defending his daughter from a stalker, Reggie approached a man's Tahoe as the man drew a gun. Reggie shot the man in the stomach several times, putting him permanently in a wheelchair and saving who knows how many girls from a terrible entrapment and fate. Of all the inmates I have met, he is the one who should not have gone to prison. Anyway, after Reggie was released, I went to visit him at his home. I met his family and his wife, Kathy. They were a typical Utah family, lived in a modest house that Reggie had grown up in. It was a far cry from the home they owned and lifestyle they had lived before Reggie was convicted.

Prior to prison, Reggie had been a very successful accountant. He had multiple employees and many large accounts, several overseas. They were livin' the dream, or so it seemed. When he was arrested, they exhausted all of their financial resources to try to mount a defense that might keep him out of prison. Now, rather than living in a lavish home in one of the leading areas of the Salt Lake Valley, they live humbly and happily in a modest home in a small town in rural Utah.

As I sat in their living room, we visited about the entire experience: the good and the bad. It was interesting to hear their experience from Kathy's perspective and learn some things about the situation that were rather personal. As the conversation progressed, I asked Kathy how she felt about Reggie having been convicted and serving 5 years in prison. Her response came surprisingly quick, "I'm thankful for it," she said. I was surprised but not completely shocked at her answer. She went on to explain that there were things about it that were miserable and almost unbearable but in a strange way it had been a blessing. Myself, I can't imagine how my wife would feel if I was sentenced to prison, guilty or not, justifiable or not. But she explained that the experience had been an eye opener and helped both of them realize what was really important in life.

I had asked the same question of Reggie earlier in the day and his response was similar. He was glad for the realizations it had brought into his life and the change of path it had set him on. No longer was he consumed with wealth and distinction. His focus was to enjoy each day with his family. Oh, he felt horrible he had put his wife and family through the ordeal but knew it had helped him grow and change immeasurably. He even mentioned the fact that he had forgiven a less-than-straightforward prosecutor, who several years earlier, he had expressed contempt for. To both of them, prison had been an unwelcomed blessing.

A second story involves a younger man named Jack . He was in his early 30's when he came to prison. Now more than 5 years later he is on parole, living in his parents' home, working in the construction industry. I had first come to meet Jack about a year into his 5-years served. He wanted to work in Education, a common desire among inmates at CUCF at the time. The general prison population came to realize that if they qualified and came to work for CUA or

228

UPrep that they were-accepted, treated well, and given responsibility and accountability. However, like some inmates, he came without leaving behind the chip on his shoulder. When he came, several of the members on our council didn't want me to hire him. He was at that point unchanged. He had a cynical type attitude at times and seemed a little entitled.

We put him to work in the copy room and as things would have it, I soon hired him to be in charge of developing UPrep; a decision not shared and appreciated by all the stake holders. UPrep was our post high school program that was just getting off the ground. For some time we had been working to get UPrep going. I had previously hired an inmate UPrep director who had failed miserably.

I looked at other options but found none. I knew, to be successful, UPrep needed the right kind of inmate leader. I was looking for someone who would take the program on his shoulders, be innovative in developing new courses, bring in new ideas and could relate with the general population of inmates to encourage them to achieve educational and behavioral compliance and also fill our classes.

I watched Jack for several months and saw in him the characteristics we needed to have a successful program. He was young and energetic with intelligence and charisma. He was well respected among the inmates and except for a bit of an attitude, or perhaps because of it, had what I was looking for. Over the next 5 years, I watched as he grew into himself. Through his efforts, we created a program that, at its peak, involved more than 100 inmate volunteers and more than 280 students. We offered courses in everything from basic study skills to accredited courses like Math 1050 and History 1700 offered by Snow College and Salt Lake Community College. It was exciting. The success of the program fell directly on Jack as a result of his personal growth. That change was the catalyst that propelled UPrep into a very successful opportunity.

The thing that was the most exciting for me in the whole experience was the change in Jack. He "came to himself." He had come from a good family and his demise had been like most inmates, Sex and Drugs and Rock-n-Roll. Now he is well on the road to recovery.

At any rate, after he paroled, my wife and I visited him and his parents in their home in southern Utah. After a very nice evening, I asked him the question, "are you glad you went to prison?" I know the answer to that question four years earlier would have been "HELL NO!" However, now the answer was an emphatic "Yes!" He was not glad he had committed his crimes. He was sorry he had hurt people and disappointed people and ruined his life and the lives of so many others. But for himself, he was glad for his time served. It had changed him, or better put, it had helped him "come to himself" and set himself back on a good path.

It is very unlikely any of that would have been the case if not for the opportunity for change given him to work and develop himself through the UPrep program. The philosophy, the company, the purpose, the hope, all contributed to helping him to no longer be "fit for prison."

Now he is in the process of working his way back into a good life. It is a difficult process. He is working hard and serving and loving and producing. It is good to see.

I have heard similar stories from dozens of other inmates I came to know. Obviously not all those incarcerated have the same experience. In fact, most don't. However, the ones who do, the ones who are glad they came to prison, are no longer "fit for prison."

The last person I would like to discuss in this example is myself. I am so thankful I was sent to prison. Let me explain. In the beginning of this book, I briefly described how I was "sentenced" to CUA. I had enjoyed a lively and fulfilling career as a high school basketball coach, teacher and administrator. I was "Livin' the Dream." I never had any intention of being the principal of a school inside a prison. I signed up to help young people through the struggles of being a teenager. I did not sign up to help the dregs of society. They deserved nothing and I certainly didn't want to give them any of my valuable time or resources.

After being sentenced by board members, I begrudgingly came to realize that there was, in prison, an opportunity to make a difference. Within about six months, my attitude changed dramatically and we went to work trying to make that difference. It has been a very enjoyable and life changing journey. I have met hundreds of people I would never have met. I have learned lessons from people that I never would have learned. I have helped people who before, I didn't think were worthy of my help. I have come to realize that God loves all His children, both those on the "outs" and those that are "down." The key difference in all people is where they are headed. Are they headed towards good things; serving, helping, giving? Or are they headed towards bad things; victimizing, begrudging, taking? I have come to realize that you don't judge a man by the color of his jumpsuit or uniform but by the content of his character, by his desire to help and lift others, by his willingness to serve and strengthen and salve wounds. By his desire to constantly change for the better, which is what we're all here to do.

I can honestly say that I have forgiven those people who sent me here. To this day, I know I did not deserve it. However, I am so thankful that this happened. I am so glad I was sent to prison. It has changed my life and hopefully, I have helped change the lives of so many of the downtrodden and outcasts of society.

Sadly, if real, lasting change is to be made in Corrections, much more needs to be done.

Chapter 29

A real solution

Choice, not chance, determines destiny.
Coach Mike Krzyzewsky

Creating a model in CUCF

For the sake of illustration, I would like to outline a scenario in which the ASCENT Tier Program for Inmates to Earn the Right to Parole could be applied and carried out at CUCF, a facility with which I have integral knowledge.

Tier 1 if not carried out in Draper, could be easily carried out in one of the sections in the Elm, housing unit. R&O is currently held there and this would be the likely location. There are three units in Elm and one unit would provide space to allow Tier 1. It would require one or more Case Workers to be assigned to mark their progress and mentor them on their journey. If an inmate progresses adequately, he could be moved to Tier 2 and start the rehabilitation process. If they fail to make any efforts, and it is clear they are not interested in making any, they can be returned to Draper, or another facility and live in general population there until they … come to themselves.

As inmates progress to Tier 2, space could be made available in one of the other sections in ELM or perhaps they could be moved to the CEDAR housing unit in the Henries. There they would progress through the self-identification part of the process. Still, spending 21 hours locked in their cell, they would be required to read self-help books from a selected list to begin their process of realizing there is a better way to live. There they would participate in physical activity in the yard as well as participate in role-playing exercises and games to help them see their behavior. Those games would be conducted by Tier 5 and 6 inmates and supervised by security staff.

This Tier will take a minimum of 3 months with no real maximum. Failure to work towards their goals may reduce their PML and may result in their being returned to Tier 1.

Tier 3, which would be considered a new type of general population, is only allowed when inmates move successfully through Tier 2 and demonstrate a real desire to grow and change. This general population would be much different than current general population. Tier 3 would be contained in several specific housing unit, perhaps BIRCH and ASPEN. There, inmates will continue to explore self-help books on a consistent basis. In addition, they will begin to explore the 12-step program and will start to explore options for employment within the prison as well as mapping a path to create reasonable employment options in prison and for the future in the community. Education, when lacking, will be a requirement for this portion of the exercise. Pending education eligibility, prison employment will be an option.

Tier 4 is also part of general population and may or may not be contained in one housing unit. During this phase, inmates will expand on tiers 2 and 3. They will delve deep into many of the Programming courses currently offered with an effort to legitimize and personalize the content. This will be done by using Tier 5 and 6 inmates as facilitators with Corrections supervision. The courses' rigor and intensity will be increased and successful completion rather than just "taking the course" will be required. Adaptations will be necessary to create a more suitable and successful learning environment.

Tier 4 will continue the educational piece as needed and will allow qualified inmates to participate in the UPrep program. This begins preparation for real employment once parole is achieved. The UPrep program will be expanded and provide, through various existing post-secondary institutions, quality and valuable education.

Tier 5 inmates will be housed in either the Gale housing unit or in the Ironwood housing unit. Completing Tier 5 is a **minimum** requirement for parole. In Tier 5, inmates spend a portion of their week volunteering their help with Tier 3 and 4 inmates. They may also hold a job and participate in any of the higher functioning activities in the facility. They begin to give back through serving as mentors to lower tier inmates.

Tier 6 inmates will also be housed in either the Gale or Ironwood housing units. They may also live in Birch or Aspen as their wishes and needs arise. Some of these inmates may be Life Without Parole (LWOP) who choose to stay to themselves or who have found that serving in Education or Programming or some other capacity is preferable. Tier 6 inmates will also volunteer some of their time as mentors and give back through the various options available to them.

After their debt to society has been paid as determined by their sentence, inmates are not considered eligible for early release, or parole, until they have spent time equivalent to their minimum sentence working through the tier system and achieving a minimum Tier 5 status and maintaining that status for a minimum period of time.

If an inmate starts down the tier path and regresses, he may be required to restart his minimum time clock. Infractions would include those things considered to be writeups, but exclude any writeups of a frivolous nature or anything resembling a quota.

I don't know that this model could be enacted at Draper. From a distance there seems to be a great disconnect in their processes and a definite difference in the culture and attitudes of personnel.

This is only an outline. Exact implementation would require a much longer conversation working with multiple entities including the state legislature to enact a change in parole requirements.

PROPOSED TIER PROGRAM

INDIVIDUAL INMATES
EARN THE RIGHT TO PAROLE

General Description

This is an outline of a tier program set forth by the Ascent Education and Employment
Committee which I was a part of from August 2016 through May 2017. The partial list of the people who sat on that committee includes: Captain Anderson later replaced on the committee by Captain Scott Crowther, Ashlea Hansen, Damon Parcell, Elaine Peterson, Gwen Solum, Jeff Tanner, Kurt Gunner, Alan James, Carlos Rodriguez, Mary Crawford, Mike Baker, Tammy Black, Tim Evans, Stephanie Patton, and Todd Bird. These individuals came from the UDOC, Education programs within UDOC, and local business owners.

The original ideas for this proposed tier program came from the original Ascent Symposium where Gordon Swensen, Director of Statewide Strategic Alliances and Initiatives, presented it to the group. We used it as guide to create our proposal. A proposal that was later derailed by "Captain Train Wreck."

This outline has been modified somewhat from the original version submitted in November of 2016. It now includes only information as it would relate to implementation at CUCF and county jails.

It is designed to walk an offender through the process of rehabilitation rather than simply throwing them in a pool and hoping they figure it out.

It is designed to teach the value of individual change, growth and service necessary for a person to evolve and become something better. Choice, responsibility, purpose and achievement are critical to the process.

Each tier is progressive. Advancement only occurs as the offender succeeds in his current tier as identified by individual progress, accomplishing tasks and improving behavior. An individual must petition to go up to the next tier. That request will be accompanied by the evaluation of staff from the current tier in a modified inmate review (OMR) setting.

The intent of the tier process is to systematically remove many of the behaviors and thinking errors of offenders. By the time they arrive at Tier 5, offenders will have eliminated criminal thinking and behavior and will be thinking and acting like regular, healthy individuals.

Tier 1 inmates will have no interaction with Tier 2 inmates. Neither will they have interaction with Tier 3 & 4 inmates. Tier 5 & 6 inmates will have some interaction, as sponsors and mentors, with Tier 2, 3 & 4 inmates but will live in separate units/sections. Concerns such as security, STG, etc. will always take precedence when housing is considered.

This entire process will be monitored by a database similar to the one used currently by CUA. All inmate steps will be verified for progression from tier to tier through WEBTrack.

To be successful, inmates must take an active role in the process.

It is important to note that this is not an entitlement program nor can it work if the inmate is not left to work his way through the program. Like any social program, the programs that don't work consist of handouts and entitlements. The programs that do work rely on ingenuity, successes mixed with failures, time, personal effort, etc. To use an applicable saying, "Give a man a fish and he eats for a day, teach him to fish and he can eat for a lifetime."

There is no maximum timetable to any tier. Occasionally there are minimum time requirements. It is a matter of individual progression and need.

Parole will only be granted to successful completers.

Inmates can be regressed to previous tiers as deemed necessary by staff according to individual behavior and effort.

A **huge** piece to the success of this idea is that one part of the UDC exists as it currently does. Officers are a vital part of dealing with offenders. By no means should Correctional officers in blue uniforms fail to perform their duties as they now exist. They must maintain control and provide punitive consequences for improper behavior. However, as inmates progress through the tier system, they will require less and less officer control and interaction. This is the Department of Prison's side.

A Department of Corrections side of the equation needs to be implemented. Two separate groups need to work together to create a learning scenario, one with a stick and one with a carrot. A learning environment must be applied in which progress through the system requires learning, growth and demonstrated outcomes but also allows for setbacks and failures. An inmate can move forward as they comply, inside and out. They will be set back as they fail to do so.

TIER ONE – Observation and Assessment, Detox (Current but with more detailed individual assessment and planning R&O)

Purpose: Realization of a need to change. Motivation to develop a desire to change

- R&O
- Take TABE test

- 23-hour lockdown
- Chemical detox completed
- Pre LSRR completed
- Develop a Comprehensive Rehabilitation Plan (CRP) that can be checked off by "certified" staff along the way, from tier to tier.
  - o Orient the inmate on exactly what must be accomplished to move from tier to tier and be eligible for parole.
- Each inmate will require an individual plan. However, common "plan templates" can and will likely exist for common personalities, crimes, and needs.
- *REQUIREMENT TO MOVE TO NEXT TIER*
  - o *As it currently exists.*

TIER TWO – Program Entry (Post R&O, segregated area, new process)
Purpose: Reinforcing the identified need to change. Creating opportunities to learn and practice proper social behavior. Beginning the process of internal improvement. Individuals will begin to remove convict mentality.

- 21-hour lockdown (not including group activities)
- Individuals create a plan similar to current STRIVE program
- 3 hours of recreation time (preferably outside) as per plan
  - o Mandatory Calisthenics (may require doctor's ok)
  - o Mandatory one-on-one game playing (physical, mental, etc.)
  - o Mandatory self-reflective studies
    - ▪ Freedom Behind Bars
    - ▪ Seven Habits

- How to Win Friends and Influence People
- As a Man Thinketh,
- Real Love
- Etc.
- If intellectual/educational levels prohibit this, it well be replaced by audio books.
- Each course would have a specific outline and questions to be review by professionals used to identify the inmate's sincere introspection.
- (NOTE) this process will continue through Tier 7 on an individual monitored basis
- Mandatory Group Therapy using mentors from Tiers 5,6 with staff supervision, *Depending on availability and need*
- Must share openly amongst others
- Must acknowledge some accountability
- Crime-specific sessions
- Must answer specific questions about his crime asked by licensed therapist.
-

- *REQUIREMENT TO MOVE TO NEXT TIER*
  - *Read and successfully complete outline and questions regarding one (possibly two) of the approved self-help books assigned.*
    - *Assessment can be done by education staff*
  - *Minimum of 3 months*
  - *Positive response to group therapy*
    - *Must share openly amongst others*

- *Must acknowledge some accountability*
- *Must answer specific questions about his crime asked by licensed therapist.*
  - *Security concerns met*
  - *Tier 2 CRP requirements met*

TIER THREE – Rehabilitation Step 1 Education (Begin Each One Teach One model) (New general population)
Purpose: At this level, the beginning of actual change starts to come out. Inmates begin thinking about the future and taking steps to change their stars.

- Continue Group Therapy Sessions
  - Develop accountability
- Begin 12-Step Program
  - Introduce sponsor (from Tier 5)
  - Bill W's "How to Work the 12-Step Program"
- Begin Education Requirements as needed
  - TABE Score improvement
  - Diploma/GED
- Continue self-reflective studies/books
- Establish Employment Re-Entry goals for Employment Index (EI)
  - Employment education requirements
  - Family related goals (reparation)
- Eligible for inmate employment as per Programming/Education/housing unit requirements.

- *REQUIREMENT TO MOVE TO NEXT TIER*
  - Read and successfully complete outline and questions regarding one (possibly two) of the approved self-help books assigned.
    - Assessment can be done by Education staff
  - Minimum of 3 months

- o Positive response to group therapy
  - ▪ Must share openly amongst others
  - ▪ Must acknowledge some accountability
  - ▪ Must answer specific questions about his crime asked by licensed therapist.
- o Education levels met
  - ▪ TABE scores
  - ▪ GED/Graduation
- o Security concerns met
- o Tier 2 CRP requirements for this level met

TIER FOUR – Rehabilitation Step 2 Programming (Use Each One Teach One model) (Current general population) Will occur simultaneously with Tier Three

Purpose: This is the tier at which individuals use group Programming to delve into their past and start seeing ways to change their future. Individuals must start seeing people as people and not as objects. They must begin learning to serve others rather than victimize others. Some elements of criminal thinking may continue but that should be discouraged both by the Programming taking place and their peers.

- ▪ Programming Classes (as needed for CAP)
  - o Keys to Loving Relationships
  - o Thinking for a Change
  - o MRT
  - o How to Win Friends and Influence People
  - o Victim Impact
  - o 12 Step Meetings
  - o Relapse Prevention
  - o Anger Management
  - o Addiction Recovery
    - ▪ HOPE, CONQUEST, etc.
  - o Journal Writing

- Mandatory weekly for entire rest of stay
  - Etc.

(NOTE) These classes need to be revitalized. They need to be real classes allowing inmates to make real associations. Using the "each one teach one" model will be critical. Standards must be set for acceptable completion of the courses. (ie course homework, tests etc.) <u>Courses should be taught by individuals</u> from Tiers 5 & 6 (mentors) with correction staff supervising and directing.

- Begin Post Secondary Education
  - Based on TABE scores
  - Based on Employment Re-Entry Goals
- Continue Group Therapy
  - Must be topic specific
    - How do you feel about your future support group?
    - Classify your family
    - Who do you want to be?
    - What has the impact been on your victims?
    - Etc.
  - The Offender must begin talking about his crime in a productive way rather than in a criminal way. How he feels about it. How he feels about his changes and future success. By now, we need to have cracked the protective surface of the offender's vulnerability. We must get through this or we cannot rehabilitate.
  - Must begin the process of seeing people as people rather than objects.
- Introduce voluntary employment (community service)

- Eligible for employment as per Programming/Education/housing unit requirements.
- Begin out of section work
  o Education Tutor
  o Programming Tutor
  o Culinary
  o Laundry
  o Maintenance
  o Etc.
- Should move into corresponding as closely as possible to desired employment upon release
- *REQUIREMENT TO MOVE TO NEXT TIER*
  o *Read and successfully complete outline and questions regarding one (possibly two) of the approved self-help books assigned (much of this evaluation will be done by mentors from tiers 5&6*
  o *Complete LSRR and show acceptable progress*
  o *Complete CAP and or show measurable progress with CAP*
  o *Willingness and cooperation in participating in "community service"*
  o *Agreement by staff (OMR) that inmate is ready for the next TIER*
  o *Only those offenders who are thinking differently and show clear progress and ability to think and function on a new level will be allowed to proceed past this point.*

TIER FIVE – Rehabilitation Step 3 – Structured Programming (Housed in a group and separate from Tier 3&4 inmates)
Purpose: This is where inmates really get inside themselves and identify who they were and who they aspire to become.

This is the actual "change" tier where the individual accepts who they were so they can become who they desire to be.

- *Tier Five is the minimum requirement for eligibility for parole*
- Become a sponsor of someone in Tier 3
  - Continue a sponsorship assignment for the rest of the program
- Continue Group Therapy
  - Should be leading/directing therapist supervised sessions
- Begin one-on-one therapy sessions (perhaps look at programs like "Choice Center" etc. for support)
  - This is where the most work will be done
  - Must open up about "demons" etc.
  - Must begin discussing them during group sessions
  - Duration dependent upon progress.
  - Corrections staff must treat these inmates as unique, belonging to a more progressive tier
  - Must identify character flaws
  - Must identify weaknesses that destroy their life
  - Graduates must be able to
    - Show remorse
    - Be accountable
    - Be willing to mentor change in others because they themselves have changed
  - Make current programs real and effective
- Commence/continue job training/post-secondary Education

TIER SIX Rehabilitation Step 4 Continued Education and Employment (Tier 6 inmates housed separate from all other inmates)

Purpose: By this point, individuals must reach the point where they can be treated and trusted like any employee. If they can't, they shouldn't be allowed to Tier 6. If they arrive and criminal behavior is still present in an offender, he is removed and sent back to whichever tier "fits" his needs. By this point, offenders need to be honest, transparent, productive, service-oriented individuals. Through their behavior at this level, we will be able to easily evaluate character. If we can't trust individuals to behave at this point, how can we let them out of prison?

- By this point, inmates MUST be developed to the point that they can be trusted to perform and behave. Trust but verify.
- Continue to volunteer and mentor
- This is a huge part of parole potential evaluation. If they can't think, act, and be trusted similar to an employee on the street, they are not ready for parole.
  - Convict mentality must be gone
  - These inmates must be given opportunity to run the programs hand-in-hand with staff
- Possibility of parole
  - Must have acceptable
    - Education Index
    - Sociability Index
  - Develop a re-entry plan
- Begin a trade
  - UCI - use to prepare for future employment
    - Expand
    - Make connections to transition
    - Could involve work release in some cases
    - Could involve county jails/IPP
  - Night School – Continue Education
    - Trade Specific
    - Directed to future employment

- - Continued from what began in Tier 3 & 4
- 5-year plan
  - o Financial planning, savings, bill consolidation
  - o Support Groups
  - o Continued education goals
    - - Certifications/Degrees
  - o Continued Therapy
  - o Sponsor/Mentor
  - o Re-Entry to family visitations
  - o Future Housing
    - - Required
      - • May exist where a positive family environment is present.
      - • If not available, program housing is a must
  - o Future Employment
    - - Required
      - • May use existing where positive relationships are present
      - • If not available, program employment is a must
- Once a parole date is offered, it is conditional upon continued progress and success.

TIER SEVEN – RE-ENTRY –Transition (Parole)
Purpose: To allow for the successful re-entry of all paroled inmates into society through an organized, integrated, purposeful process. AP&P will oversee Tier 7 progress
- - Individual Transition Plans will have been developed in Tier 6 and will be used to transition into Tier 7

- For any of these transition programs, compliance through completion is a requirement for continued parole.
- Individuals must apply and be accepted into each program
- Each parolee will have a mentor as well as a parole officer
- The Other Side Academy model
- UDOWD
- IPS
- Halfway houses
    o Must make accountable
    o Must use prior SUCCESSFUL offenders as mentors
- Employment Partners
    o Will take active role in monitoring progress
- Connection to SATP, SOTP, etc. support groups will be made in conjunction with AP&P, IPS, etc.
- Stay away lists
    o People
    o Substances
    o Locations
- Fitted with tracking device as deemed necessary
- As with all Tiers in this outline, time for each parolee is dependent on individual success and progress.

JUSTIFICATION

Our system completely fails society and inmates by releasing them without any real support or education. Though best efforts are made everywhere in the current situation, there is no real process in place.

It took most of these men **years** to get where they are. It is reasonable to expect it would take years to change them. The violin analogy given at the ASCENT symposium is a perfect example of what is required to provide opportunity for change. Just like the violin, an individual must **want to learn** to play. They must **receive proper training**. They must **practice, fail and try again**. They must **receive more support and instruction**. They must **play in front of others** and learn to deal with that pressure. They must have a **continual desire to improve**. They must **feel good about their process**. They must be, over extended time, taught and **prepared to perform in public**. Parole should be the climax of a process of change, similar to a violin recital. *Expecting a parolee to perform as a citizen without the necessary preparation is exactly like asking someone to play a violin concert without preparation.* Failure will be eminent.

People want to be better. People want to perform. People want to be productive. Many people just don't know how. Let them buy into the process. Let them realize they have a chance. Provide them **real hope**. They will **choose** to change.

Implemented, this process will be less expensive and more productive. Our recidivism rates will drop.

It will not apply to all inmates. But we can be confident that paroled inmates will see dramatic positive results.

If an inmate refuses to take the steps before him, he chooses to serve out his complete sentence. As they choose to change and take advantage of the opportunities before them, we will have moved much closer to finding lasting solutions for individuals as well as society.

Biography

Mark Hugentobler

Mark Hugentobler graduated Magna Cum Laude from Weber State College in 1984 with a BS in Mathematics, Physical Science and Computer Technology and later graduated Cum Laude with a Master's from Utah State University in Gifted and Talented Education. Shortly after that, he received his Administrative Endorsement from Utah State University. For over 25 years he worked as a high school teacher and coach. During that time, he taught algebra and coached Cross County and Basketball. With Cross Country for 11 years, his teams won the state championships in 1988 and 1993. Coaching basketball, Mark's teams earned State Titles in 1996, 2003 and 2008 as well as winning multiple regional titles. Mark's work in the classroom has also been recognized. He was considered a master teacher through most of his tenure. In 2010 he received the KSL Teacher Feature award and then in 2018 was honored by the state adult education association, UAACCE as the Outstanding Adult Educator. Mark has always appreciated the many young (and more recently older) people he has worked with over the years and credits them for his successes. Mark is very active in his church. He and his wife, Angie, live in central Utah and are the parents of 5 children.

Made in the USA
San Bernardino, CA
21 June 2020